anti-capitalism

a beginner's guide

anti-capitalism

a beginner's guide

simon tormey

ONEWORLD
OXFORD

anti-capitalism: a beginner's guide

Oneworld Publications
(Sales and Editorial)
185 Banbury Road
Oxford OX2 7AR
England
www.oneworld-publications.com

ISBN 1–85168–342–9

Cover design by the Bridgewater Book Company
Typeset by Jayvee, Trivandrum, India
Printed and bound by Thomson Press (India) Ltd

contents

four   a 'movement of movements' ii: renegades, radicals and revolutionaries   107

five   the future(s) of anti-capitalism: problems and perspectives   140

acknowledgements

I need, firstly, to thank the team at Oneworld for their help and guidance since the inception of this project. It has been a source of surprise, delight and fear to find publishers who took such a close interest in what I was writing. Secondly, I'd like to thank the many individuals who chipped in with ideas, read portions of what I was writing or otherwise made my life easier. I should mention in particular Pete Waterman and Graeme Chesters, both of whom came out of the blue with interesting suggestions, papers and bibliographies. Easily my largest debt in this regard is, however, owed to Andy Robinson. As well as supplying a near constant stream of activist materials over the past few years, he has been a valuable 'sounding-board' for more or less every idea or theme that has found its way into the book. He also read and commented – in his own inimitable fashion – on crucial parts of the manuscript. Finally, I'd like to thank Véronique and our children, Max, Gabrielle and Louis for putting up with me and my numerous 'absences' when I should have been reading them a book or playing in the field.

This book is dedicated to the original anarcho-situationist-beatnik, my mother, Patricia Tormey. Some are given to write and think about life 'after' capitalism, and some already live it.

introduction

'beginning' anti-capitalism

Those who write about contemporary radical politics, whether mainstream or 'activist', agree that something new was born at the Seattle protests against the World Trade Organisation (WTO) in December 1999. This was a global movement variously termed 'anti-capitalist', 'anti-globalisation', 'anti-corporate', 'anti-neoliberal'. Now the movement is often referred to – and refers to itself – in more 'positive' terms, that is, as the 'Movement for Global Justice' or the 'Global Justice and Solidarity Movement' (being just two examples). All these labels point to the same people, the same groups, the same events and protests, though the proliferation of labels gives an indication of why it is that people are often confused about what it stands for or what it represents. Confusing though the picture may be, this is not to say that there is little to read on the subject. A great deal has *already* been written about the movement, so much so that it is legitimate to ask why we need yet another book on what must be one of the most written about phenomena of recent years. Why do we need *Anti-Capitalism: A Beginner's Guide*? What can I hope to add to what is already a mountain of often informed, sometimes entertaining, and just occasionally wearisome writing on the subject?

As someone who has been teaching a variety of 'anti-capitalist' subjects for two decades I have at least attempted to keep up with most things 'anti-capitalist' over the course of that time. This was a fairly straightforward task until 1999. Before then, 'anti-capitalism' meant looking mostly at the ideas and events of the past, sometimes the far-flung past. It also meant keeping abreast of the various activisms and ways in which deeply unfashionable ideas like 'socialism', 'anarchism' and 'Marxism' were supposed to be evolving,

1

changing or adapting to 'New Times'. 'Anti-capitalism' was a minority subject, in this case a very minor one compared with my colleagues who have interests in 'liberalism' or 'conservatism'. 1999 changed all that. What we have witnessed since Seattle is an enormous outpouring of analyses, commentaries, manifestos all to go alongside the huge increase in activist materials, websites, newspapers and periodicals. It has been an immensely exciting period, particularly for those who thought the emergence of a genuinely global anti-capitalist movement was unlikely, to say the least. Looking at the mountain of material out there what is noticeable is that the work of those committed to saying something or writing about anti-capitalism tends to be of three kinds, some of which may be helpful *to* beginners, but few of which are *for* beginners. It will be useful to say something about what has been written so far, if only to give the reader a sense of what is already available, and also a sense of how I see my own task in relation to the existing literature on the subject.

Firstly, there are books that are what might be termed *activist orientated*. This is to say they are either written by activists *about* activism or written by activists *for* other activists (or would-be activists). These include the useful *Anti-Capitalism: A Guide to the Movement*. This is a cheap, well-produced account of the issues and events surrounding the birth of the anti-capitalist movement. It is published under the aegis of the British Socialist Workers' Party (SWP), and many (though not all) of those writing commentaries or chapters are members of the Party. Those who are not are all activists of one kind or another and are able to give a good sense of the movement, where it has come from and where it is going. It is a good place to go for facts as well as a politically committed survey of developments. We can also mention the collections *Another World is Possible: Popular Alternatives to Globalization at the World Social Forum* edited by William Fisher and Thomas Ponniah; *There Is an Alternative: Subsistence and Worldwide Resistance to Corporate Globalization* edited by Veronika Bennholdt-Thomsen; and *Globalization from Below* edited by Jeremy Brecher, Tim Costello, and Brendan Smith. Best of all the collections is probably *We are Everywhere: The Irresistible Rise of Global Anticapitalism*, produced by the 'Notes from Nowhere' collective. This is to say nothing at all about the reams of activist material in activist outlets. Indeed, if one really wants to get the 'worm's eye view' of what the anti-capitalist movement means to those who are part of it, then it would be indispensable to consult materials such as these.

Secondly, there are what might be termed *expert analyses*. These are works by people who have conducted research on some aspect or another of the contemporary global situation, together with a critique of it. The most notable of these would be the various writings of Naomi Klein. Her book *No Logo* is the outstanding recent contribution of its kind, and is rightly hailed as one of the key works helping to unpack the issues behind the corporate domination of the global market-place. She has also published a set of essays, *Fences and Windows*, a collection of many of the articles she has published with various newspapers and journals in the wake of the Seattle protests. Another 'early' work that caught the eye of a supposedly indifferent public is Noreena Hertz's *The Silent Takeover*, an analysis of the ways in which corporate power is 'silently' undermining democratic decision-making. We also need to mention the work of Noam Chomsky, perhaps the single most penetrating critic of liberal-democratic politics of the past four decades. I list a number of his works at the end of chapters, but readers can note that the *Zmag.org* website carries up-to-date interviews with Chomsky, which are perhaps the best way in which the beginner can get a sense of where he stands on the key issues of the day. There are other works by investigative journalist-cum-activists that are also expert in this sense. Many will be familiar with the works of Michael Moore who like Klein has done much, particularly in North America, to accentuate the issues surrounding US corporate domination of the world's economy and also the obstacles to the emergence of a progressive politics in his own country. We can also mention the work of Gregory Palast, whose *The Best Democracy Money Can Buy* is, like the work of Moore, a stinging exposé of the nature of American politics. There are also various collections or readers which collate the work of a number of experts. The best of those currently available is *The Anti-Capitalism Reader: Imagining a Geography of Opposition* edited by Joel Shalit. It too has a US-focus. It has the merit of bringing together not only well-known critics of global capitalism like Walden Bello and Doug Henwood, and also giving room to those with a variety of critical perspectives. Probably the most detailed 'expert' account of the anti-capitalist movement itself – particularly the US movement – is Amory Starr's excellent *Naming the Corporate Enemy: Anti-Corporate Movements Confront Globalization*, a comprehensive digest of all things 'anti-corporate' together with a critical evaluation of the various strengths and weaknesses of the movement.

In view of recent developments it is unsurprising, finally, to find that there is now a burgeoning literature of *anti-capitalist advocacy*. These include outright 'manifestos' whose aim is to marshal the movement behind a particular political project or vision of how the world should look. Notable amongst these are Alex Callinicos's *An Anti-Capitalist Manifesto*, George Monbiot's *The Age of Consent*, and Colin Hines's *Localization; A Global Manifesto*. We should also mention Paul Kingsnorth's *One No, Many Yeses*, though it combines elements of all three approaches listed above, being an activist ramble around various sites of struggle, a useful overview of the issues and a modest manifesto for 'revolution'. This is, however, just the tip of the iceberg. It is no exaggeration to say that every group, party or sub-movement within the movement has its own manifesto or 'programme' for making the world a better, fairer, cleaner, happier place. We should also add that many of those books listed under other headings have their own 'agenda', sometimes explicit, sometimes less so. All this is to be expected. Most books about anti-capitalism will tell us something about the author's preferences; why else would they be moved to write at all?

So there is plenty to read out there. Why then do we need another book? As someone who spends a lot of time thinking, teaching and writing about anti-capitalism in one form or another, what is apparent is that there is nothing (yet) I could put in the hand of an undergraduate student, a curious friend, relative or neighbour and say 'here, this is quite a lot of what you might need to know about contemporary anti-capitalism. Here is an overview of the issues involved, together with a digest of some of the key arguments and issues to be found in the movement'. This is to say there is nothing much for the *beginner* either in the sense of someone who wants merely to understand what is going on, or in the sense of someone who wants to begin but doesn't 'know' *where* to 'begin'. Here a word or two is needed about the notion of 'beginner' underpinning the book.

I have thought hard about 'the beginner' to try to ensure that I keep within the remit of what my publishers want, but also because in a subject like this the notion of a beginner is ambiguous, handily so in the case of a 'political' topic like anti-capitalism. 'Beginners' can be passive or they can be active. They can, that is, be seeking merely to find out more about the anti-capitalist movement, why it came about, who's in it, where it's all heading. On the other hand they might be thinking 'something must be done', and be asking themselves where to find out 'more' about the various resistances and campaigns going on. This is (hopefully) a book for both kinds of 'beginner'. This is to say that it is not an 'idiot's guide', nor is it an 'Anti-Capitalism 101' exercise. 'Beginners' are not 'idiots', nor are they necessarily students who have been told to go away and look something up about anti-capitalism for the purpose of writing a paper or giving a presentation to a class. On the other hand, 'idiots' (in the sense used in the context of the ubiquitous 'Idiot's Guides', that is, someone who knows *nothing* about a subject) and students *may* and often are beginners in the sense used here.

I should say one more thing about the 'beginner' and how it informs the kind of book I wanted to write. In my experience as a teacher beginners to a subject do not want to be told what the answers are, so much as what the *issues* are. They want a guide to a controversy, the ideology, the movement, the 'territory' so that they can find their own way around in 'it'. The worst teaching experiences I have endured (and indeed been responsible for) are those where an 'expert' wears her politics 'on her sleeve'. I don't like being harangued about a subject, told what to think, or how to respond, and nor do most of those I have tried to help learn about a subject. This is not to say that I am 'neutral' on the subject of anti-capitalism, as if one could be indifferent to the issues we will be discussing. I am not – and it will not take long for the reader to work out where I am coming from. Nonetheless, for the purpose of this book I have at least aimed at providing a *map* of the issues that will be of relevance to the interested beginner, not a set of *directions* pointing her to the 'right' place. This is not an activist work for activists; nor is it a manifesto or guide on how to change the world. It is a work by a specialist, but it is not an 'expert' analysis in the sense used above. I am not, that is, presenting new research or fieldwork designed to expose global inequities. What I have aimed for is a guide to the issues, positions, alternatives. So what is it that needs to be mapped? Before plunging in, let's review how the book unfolds. This will enable those with some idea of the nature of anti-capitalism to decide what to read and what to skip over.

Chapter 1 concerns the nature of capitalism, what it is, where it is going and how we are 'sold' it. This already sounds odd. Why start a book on anti-capitalism with an excursus on the nature of capitalism? As will become apparent, one of the key assumptions underpinning the book is that the world is as it is not because it has to be, but because a group of individuals *want* it to be that way. In wanting a certain state of affairs to continue they give reasons or arguments why it should be left alone. Part of the task anti-capitalists set for themselves is to show that these reasons are poor ones. Assuming they succeed then the assumption is that people will change their minds about the virtues of capitalism. If enough people change their minds then, so most activists argue, we could contemplate living in a different kind of world. All of which presupposes that we understand what it is that those who defend it think is superior about capitalism as a system and as a basis for global politics. This is not to say that the reason why we have a capitalist world order is because most people find these arguments convincing. Clearly, one of the problems that besets global politics is that most people do not get asked what their opinion is of the matter. Capitalism is just *there* – like it or not. Nonetheless, from the point of view of appreciating anti-capitalist positions it is useful to know *why* it is there, why it takes the form that it does and how it is that contemporary capitalism can come to seem just and reasonable, as it does to many ordinary men and women. This is our task in chapter one.

In *Chapter 2* we look at the factors that led to the emergence of the anti-capitalist movement. We begin by looking at how it is that commentators seem to have been caught unawares by the explosive emergence of what is now a genuinely *global* movement. We then move to a consideration of the factors themselves, looking in particular at the legacy of 1968 for the kind of politics we see today. We look in particular at the emergence of alternatives to Soviet Marxism, the significance of the Paris uprising in terms of prefiguring a different kind of politics, and also the emergence of the so-called new social movements and 'single issue politics'. I then try to explain how it was that a process characterised by the fragmentation of radical energies could coalesce around an anti-capitalist 'pole'. Here we discuss the identification of a common enemy, namely corporations and neoliberalism more generally; the emergence of the internet as a basis for a new form of 'network' politics; and the possibility of global dialogue, leading to the creation of a global movement.

In *Chapters 3 and 4* we look at the various anti-capitalist arguments, positions, groups and critiques themselves. In chapter three we look at the position of the 'reformists', those who are committed to altering global capitalism, but not transforming or abolishing it. This encompasses a range of positions from what we term liberal interventionism to global social democracy. In chapter four we look at the radical wing of anti-capitalism, in other words those who are committed to a fundamental change in the world. We begin with an overview of Marxist positions. We then move on to consider various autonomist currents and the position of the anarchists. We also look at the radical wing of environmentalism, including groups such as Earth First! and the primitivists. The chapter concludes with a discussion of 'Zapatismo', the current of radical thought associated with the Zapatistas in Mexico.

In the final chapter, *Chapter 5*, we consider the prospects for the anti-capitalist 'movement of movements'. We begin by looking at the 'external' factors that may shape the options and strategies of anti-capitalists. These include the position of the US in global politics and also the changing nature of transnational capitalism. The bulk of the chapter consists of an assessment of the factors that may determine the future course of anti-capitalist initiatives. As well as considering the problem of steering a movement that is composed of a vast diversity of different ideologies, positions, groups and visions, we also look closely at the dynamics of such a movement. We focus in particular on the different logics or tendencies of political organisation, contrasting the 'network' approach often favoured by more direct action orientated activists with the more traditional 'vertical' structures favoured by the anti-capitalist 'mainstream' – if this isn't too odd an expression.

An essential task of anyone aiming to be of genuine use to a beginner is to provide information on *resources*. Readers will find that relevant sources to information mentioned in the course of the book are placed at the end of each chapter. This includes books and articles, and also web addresses for relevant organisations and groups. I have also included a timeline for giving some sense of how the anti-capitalist phenomenon has unfolded. There is a glossary of key terms, thinkers and institutions as well. The web is an indispensable source generally for finding out about anti-capitalism, learning more about the various groups and activisms out there, and indeed for getting involved. I have provided a handful of suggestions for links, despite the fact that they have a tendency to go 'dead' and otherwise embarrass those recommending them. I have also listed a number of articles and texts that have URLs. Many of these are out-of-copyright 'classics' and can be found somewhere, even if the particular URL supplied has gone out of date. In all cases, if there is a problem with a link, try typing the full author/title information into a reputable search engine such as *Google*. It should turn up somewhere. There is, in any case, *no* shortage of people, groups, organisations out there who share an interest at the nature and fate of anti-capitalism. What I supply here is, for better or worse, just the tip of the iceberg.

resources

read on

Veronika Bennholdt-Thomsen *et al.* (eds), *There is an Alternative: Subsistence and Worldwide Resistance to Corporate Globalization* (London: Zed Books, 2001).

Emma Bircham and John Charlton (eds), *Anti-Capitalism: A Guide to the Movement* (London: Bookmarks, 2001).

Jeremy Brecher, Tim Costello, and Brendan Smith (eds), *Globalization from Below* (London: South End Press, 2001).

Alex Callinicos, *An Anti-Capitalist Manifesto* (Cambridge: Polity Press, 2003).

William Fisher and Thomas Ponniah (eds), *Another World is Possible: Popular Alternatives to Globalization at the World Social Forum* (London: Zed Books, 2003).

Noreena Hertz, *The Silent Takeover* (London: Arrow, 2002).

Colin Hines, *Localization; A Global Manifesto* (London: Earthscan, 2000).

Paul Kingsnorth, *One No, Many Yeses: A Journey to the Heart of the Global Resistance Movement* (London: Free Press, 2003).

Naomi Klein, *No Logo* (London: Flamingo, 2000).

Naomi Klein, *Fences and Windows* (London: Flamingo, 2002).

George Monbiot, *The Age of Consent* (London: Flamingo, 2003).

Michael Moore, *Downsize This!* (London: Pan, 2002).

Notes from Nowhere (ed.), *We are Everywhere: The Irresistible Rise of Global Anticapitalism* (London and New York: Verso, 2003).

Gregory Palast, *The Best Democracy Money Can Buy* (London: Robinson, 2002).

Joel Shalit (ed.), *The Anti-Capitalism Reader: Imagining a Geography of Opposition* (New York: Akashic Books, 2002).

Amory Starr, *Naming the Corporate Enemy: Anti-Corporate Movements Confront Globalization* (London, Zed Books, 2000).

link to

www.nologo.org
www.monbiot.org
www.paulkingsnorth.net
www.michaelmoore.com
www.gregpalast.com

the hows and whys of the thing called 'capitalism'

a question of definition

In a book about anti-capitalism we are naturally enough going to hear all sorts of reasons why it is that we should be opposed to capitalism. Many of these arguments will differ in sometimes surprising and indeed conflicting ways; but one thing they will all have in common is that they know what they are against: the Thing called 'Capitalism' – or, more likely, refinements of the same such as 'neoliberal capitalism', 'transnational capitalism', 'economic globalisation', 'corporate capitalism'. Whilst anti-capitalist literature is replete with reasons why one should oppose capitalism, they are often less helpful on what 'capitalism' is and how it differs from other forms of social organisation. They are often less than forthcoming, too, on why it is that capitalism is 'hegemonic', why it appears 'natural' or 'normal' to so many (as it does). Thus what the 'beginner' to the subject might already have asked him or herself is how it is that anyone came to think that capitalism was worth defending in the first place. So, thinking in terms of how to initiate the 'beginner' into the nature of anti-capitalism, it is as good a place as any to start with some brief thoughts on *capitalism* itself. In particular we need to think about how capitalism established itself as a dominant economic system, and one accepted as 'rational' and 'desirable' by many throughout both the developed and developing world.

First of all it will be helpful to think about the central term 'capitalism' itself. What exactly is capitalism? There are two ways of answering this question. The first is to think of it in *abstract* terms, that is in terms of what it represents as a relationship between people. The second is to think in more *historical* terms, i.e. of how it is that capitalism came about, and how it developed into the system we see before us today. Why do we need two ways of thinking about the same object? The easy answer is that since the dawn of capitalism in the early modern period (roughly the seventeenth century onwards) capitalism has obviously changed a great deal. Indeed it has changed so much that it is remarkable to be talking about the same 'thing' at all, the world of the twenty-first century being radically different to that of even the nineteenth century, let alone the seventeenth. Yet economists and commentators still agree for the most part that there is a fundamental continuity between the Then and the Now. What then is the continuity? Fortunately there is little controversy over the matter. 'Capitalism' is not in this sense a particularly contested term in itself. What *is* contested is whether it is just, rational or otherwise in the best interests of humanity. In *abstract* terms it is said that we have capitalism where we see the following:

- Private ownership over the means of production: land, factories, businesses.
- 'Paid employment' or, to put it another way, 'wage labour'.
- Creation of goods – or the offering of services – for profit via a system of exchange, i.e. the market.

This is a pretty anodyne definition, which is to say, that most of those who take some 'professional' interest in the matter would regard it with a shrug of the shoulders. This is what is intended. We are looking for a base line here: something that can be agreed on, so that we can understand exactly what it is that pro-capitalists celebrate and anti-capitalists object to. This is not, however, to say that everyone describes capitalism in the same way. We can note that, for example, Karl Marx, unarguably the greatest anti-capitalist thinker, analyses the two antagonistic classes produced under capitalism: the 'bourgeoisie' and the 'proletariat'. What defines the bourgeoisie is, nonetheless, the fact that they are owners of capital and usually employ others, the working class, to create profit. How Marx analyses the operation of the capitalist system actually accords closely to those of the 'bourgeois' economists he otherwise opposed, such as David Ricardo, Adam Smith and Jean Baptiste Say – as he himself was happy to confirm. Looking at the definition other questions will, however, arise. 'Beginners' as well as cynics might think that capitalism looks in this view utterly basic to human experience. What other kinds of economic relations might there be?

There is some substance to the concern, the chief among these being the relationship between capitalism and the market, or 'commodity production'. Hasn't there always been a market, and thus capitalism? The market or commodity production is indeed much older than capitalism, and there are those who would insist that virtually every society known to us embraced *some* form of market exchange, whether that be the exchange of shark teeth, beetroot or gold pieces. This is actually a very important point with respect to questions raised in relation to anti-capitalism, and so the need for clarity here is acute. The point is that the market is not an invention *of* capitalism, nor does the market of itself lead *to* capitalism. Markets have existed alongside all manner of different economic regimes and different forms of ownership. The mere exchange of 'equivalents' does not in other words necessitate or make inevitable wage labour, which is in turn the key to understanding the distinctiveness of capitalist production. A group of children swapping football stickers might be said to be entering into a market transaction in the sense that there is an exchange of equivalents. Some of the cards may be rarer than others, and so trade for higher 'value' than others. Nor is the market in this sense something new or confined to capitalist economies. Markets have existed for longer than human history itself, which is not to say that the market is inevitable or necessary to human life as such, only that markets frequently arise in the course of human interrelationships, and will probably go on doing so as long as people want to swap things like football stickers. But the point is, the market is not capitalism, and capitalism is not the market. So what is?

Looking back at the definition what becomes apparent is that one of the distinctive features of capitalism is that it serves a *particular kind* of market, namely that for labour. In pre-capitalist times labour was sometimes bought, but more often than not it was procured by some other means, classically by the institution of slavery, and more recently by bondage, vassalage, or other arrangement that rendered individuals directly subservient to someone else. In other words, through force of arms, conquest, or some other more or less violent process people were made subjects of a lord or noble. As a slave or serf a person had little or no control over his or her own life, but rather was a mere adjunct of an 'estate' to which he or she was personally tied. As feudalism and slavery were overthrown or displaced, so those who were 'liberated' became 'masterless men (and women)', freed to try and procure a living for themselves, usually through selling their labour to someone who needed it for the factories, mines and workhouses that accompanied the process of industrialisation. Here, in short, we see a process by which the economic relation of feudalism, namely control over the *person* is transformed into the capitalist economic relation in which some people buy other people's *labour power*. Whereas in the market place of Ancient Rome or of *ante bellum* America it was people who were bought and sold, in the capitalist market place it is our labour power that is bought and sold. But what is our labour power bought and sold for? Why do people need to buy and sell labour power?

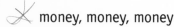

money, money, money

This brings us to the second relatively uncontroversial part of the definition of capitalism, which is that under capitalism the primary purpose of production is profit or making money. This too sounds a banal 'fact' about the way we live. What on earth could be the point of setting up companies, working hard, taking risks, indeed getting up in the morning if it was not for making money?

We shall hear quite a lot more about what other ends production *could* serve when we come to discuss anti-capitalist ideas themselves, but for the purpose of contrast we could at this point think about one possible alternative to production as profit, which is production for what is termed 'subsistence'. It is probably a truism to note that over the course of human history most economic activity has been for the purpose of maintaining the well-being of the family and the extended groups of which the individual is a part rather than for making a profit as such. Looking closely at pre-capitalist production what is striking is the degree to which people worked just enough to ensure that they have the things they need to keep them going and to ensure that as and when unexpected crises come along (bad weather, poor crops, etc.), there was enough surplus to ensure that everyone was looked after. This is what it means to subsist: a farmer works hard enough and long enough to make sure that all basic needs are met. Beyond that however, life is for living, singing songs, lazing in the sun, swimming, painting or whatever. Under such conditions 'profit' as such has little rationale. To the subsistence farmer, profit requires extra work, and extra work means less time to do the other things she or he wants to do as well. This is one of the ironies of capitalist production spotted by the very earliest critics of capitalism. We often work harder and for longer hours to be able to do the things that, if we worked less and for fewer hours, we would be able to do anyway, like lazing in the sun. So inevitably the question arises of why capitalism is characterised by production for profit as opposed to something else, like subsistence?

To answer this question we need to make a link between wage labour and profit creation, for what has yet to be clarified is why anyone would want to work for someone else rather than work for themselves as, say, a subsistence farmer. Why do most of us work for someone else, and not for ourselves, or for our families, or relatives or friends and neighbours, or with whom we choose?

Historically, the reason why most of us work for others is that we have very little choice but to do so. It is again a truism to note that in most parts of the world, *the* most important resource allowing a degree of independence to individuals, namely land, was conquered, invaded or otherwise taken from indigenous groups to serve the needs of royal families, *conquistadores*, colonial barons, imperial elites or states. In the UK the story of the creation of 'masterless men' – or future 'employees' – is one that concerns conquest of a particularly crude, and at times bloody, kind over the course of the previous three centuries, and this is to say nothing of '1066' and the Norman conquest of Britain. It was crude in the case of the 'enclosures' of the late eighteenth and early nineteenth centuries. This ensured that large chunks of the English countryside were hived off to the 'great families' in the name of 'improving' the land, that is making it available for agro-industrial development or building plots. It was bloody in the case of the 'Highland clearances' of the same period that ensured royal and noble control over the magnificent wilderness regions of Scotland. The effect was the same. Formerly independent 'subsistence' farmers were thrown off the land, in turn forcing them into the towns and cities to search for work. We can note that some of the very first 'anti-capitalist' protests and demonstrations were sparked off by such processes, and account in part for the sporadic resistances, sometimes violent, that punctuate modern British history, notwithstanding the insistence in 'official' history of the idea of Britain's 'peaceful' historical development.

This is part of the story of the industrial revolution in Britain, and it is in turn part of the story of virtually every country the world over. It is part of the story too of anti-capitalism in those countries that have experienced the failures of 'land reform' in recent times. We could mention here the case of Mexico where the Zapatista rebellion of 1994 was initiated by those seeking a return of control over scarce arable land in the mountainous Chiapas region. We could also mention the Sem Terra, or landless, of Brazil striving for the means of getting land for those who have been deprived of it, or the Via Campesina network that attempts to help various groups restore their rights to land and agricultural produce. But the story of the conquest of 'subsistence' is not the *whole* story, as those who defend capitalism will, with varying degrees of skill and urgency, insist.

Finally, we should also note that the *private* ownership of the means of production is hardly intrinsic to human experience. For much of history, hunter-gathering was the norm and where this was displaced it was often by various forms of *collective* ownership, whether by families or kinship groups, or by larger units such as villages, towns and city-states. We can also note that even under advanced industrial conditions private ownership of production existed side-by-side with public ownership, as for example in the welfare or social democratic states of the early to mid-twentieth century. Indeed as recently as the mid-1980s over 50% of French GDP was accounted for by publicly owned enterprises. Even this ratio is dwarfed by the situation that obtained in communist states such as the former Soviet Union where the vast bulk of the productive capacity of the country rested in 'collective' hands, admittedly a euphemism for the party-state apparatus that ruled the country until its collapse in 1991. The private ownership of the means of production has thus historically *supplanted* a variety of other kinds of ownership, collective, communal and feudal. It also supplanted varieties of 'non-ownership', as in hunter-gathering and nomadic forms of life that subsisted without resort to ownership over the land and natural resources. It has also *co-existed* alongside rival forms of ownership, particularly the large-scale state ownership seen in the former communist bloc. Many if not all of these alternatives have some supporters amongst anti-capitalist groups, and so we will be returning to the issue of which, if any of them, could provide a realistic and/or desirable alternative to the forms of ownership so many anti-capitalists object to.

So to summarise this brief discussion, we can talk about capitalism in abstraction from the historical conditions that brought it into being, but only just. Without some element of that history, we get the how, but we don't get the why, which is equally part of the case before us. We can see in particular that capitalism is not the *same* as the market. Capitalism *is* of course a market society, but market societies may take forms other than those found under capitalist conditions. Even feudal and slave-owning societies were 'market societies'. We can also see that capitalism requires a certain kind of social relation, namely that between 'formally free' individuals. This means that wage labour is only possible where people are free to the extent of being able to sell their own labour power to someone else. People whose labour is forcefully taken from them are formally unfree like slaves or serfs. We can also see that capitalism is about the creation of profit. Profit is needed not least to give owners the money they need to keep themselves alive. It is also needed to reinvest in their businesses, in particular in the new technology and equipment that will enable them to compete successfully with others and thereby maintain those profits without which any capitalist enterprise will fail.

capitalism as a system of competition

Though we have not mentioned it so far, this final point illustrates an important aspect of capitalism, which is that it is normally, though not necessarily, characterised by *intense competition*. Capitalism is as we know defined by the existence of a market: without a market there is no capitalism. A market is a physical or nominal 'space' in which those with something to sell or exchange – like their own labour or football stickers – can seek buyers. Much of the time there are others who will be wanting to sell something similar, and so there is a competition for buyers. What determines who wins the competition is, when all other things are equal, price. I need some tomatoes, so I go to the market and see someone selling them for 2 cents a kilo and someone else selling them for 3. They look pretty similar in size and price and so, being the 'rational' person I am, I buy my tomatoes from the former. Now the question is what determines price? This is actually a fairly vexatious question in the specialist literature. Nevertheless, it seems reasonable enough to say that whilst demand *is* important – the greater the demand, the higher the price that can be charged – the cost of production operates at the very least as a 'bottom line' beneath which the producer cannot go. Ultimately it always costs *something* to produce tomatoes and get them to the market. People have to be employed to plant the seeds, or, there again, a family has to keep itself in food and clothing in order to sow the crop; transport must be paid for, packaging, boxes, sometimes the stall itself has to be rented or bought. All of these are basic costs which have to be 'passed on' in the price of tomatoes. Let's say these basic costs amount to 20 cents per kilo. If the price of tomatoes goes below that level and stays there for very long our tomato growers are in trouble. Unless they have some reserves stashed away, or have access to some other product they will go bust.

Now what is obvious is that the lower these basic costs, the lower, potentially, one can set the price of the tomatoes. As is also obvious, tomato sellers working in a commercial context *want* to obtain as high a price as they can for their tomatoes, but they also remember that there are other tomato sellers out there competing for custom. So the tendency in market-based societies is competition on costs, *all* of the costs not just that of the labour power without which ultimately there can be no tomato farming. The seller who can reduce her costs, can reduce her prices further than the seller who has higher costs. This in turn means that in a period or environment of *intense competition* and relatively open markets, such as that found under capitalist conditions, that seller will be at an advantage: she will 'win' the competition, driving her competitors out of business, into retirement or another sector of the market. That is until another tomato grower comes along who thinks she can reduce her costs *even further* (and so on).

There is, however, another way to 'win', and that is for one tomato seller to buy out or otherwise eliminate her rivals, leaving just herself in the market place. This is the *monopoly* scenario dreaded by both pro- and anti-market theorists since the dawn of economics. If I buy out the other tomato sellers and establish myself as the only seller of tomatoes then, assuming a constant demand for tomatoes, we can anticipate that the costs of tomatoes will rise enormously, making those big profits tomato growers apparently yearn for. Monopolies are bad. They eliminate competition and inflate prices to exorbitant levels. Monopolies represent the death of the market and thus ultimately the death of capitalism. It is for this reason that virtually every defender of capitalism has argued for the necessity to ensure that monopolies are prevented from emerging. Even such stalwart defenders of the 'minimal' or *laissez-faire* state such as Adam Smith and Friedrich von Hayek were agreed on the necessity for state intervention on these grounds.

What still needs clarification, however, is the difference between capitalist and non-capitalist forms of market competition. The tomato seller example used above illustrates some of what happens in markets as such, not just *capitalist* markets. Isn't there a difference? Indeed there is. As we have had occasion to note, a key to understanding capitalism is wage labour, and thus the competition for labour between capitalists. They need us, and in the absence of other means of keeping ourselves alive like having our own land, we need them. So the cost issue that we were discussing above refers very particularly to the costs of labour power and of keeping us working. This is much less the case in pre-capitalist societies where a great deal of production is based either on enforced labour of the feudal kind or on subsistence farming and manufacture which is characterised by family or small group production, rather than on wage labour. We have also noted that production in the capitalist market is for profit, with at least some of that profit being used for increasing the level of *productivity* through investing in machinery, new technologies, plant and equipment. So capitalism is a particularly *energetic*, or perhaps frenetic form, of market society. Whereas the pre-capitalist market mainly concerns the reproduction of the basic necessities of life (give or take luxury goods for the few) the capitalist market concerns the *accumulation* of capital through the exploitation of all available means for the increasing of production, whilst at the same time diminishing costs. Under the capitalist market there is no resting place for producer *or* seller. Capitalism is in its own self-image a Darwinian struggle, a struggle with many winners and many losers. It is for this reason that even Marx paused – part in admiration, part in incredulity – at the sheer brutal relentlessness of the system, even whilst exclaiming how much he detested it.

capitalism now

So far we have been describing capitalism in fairly *abstract* terms. That is, we have been trying to extract what it is that unites the very early forms of capitalist society with what we see around us today, but what we see around us Now is very different in many ways to what existed Then. It is time to think about what these differences are so we get a better sense of the Thing that contemporary anti-capitalism seeks to oppose. This means thinking further about:

- Interdependence and the transnationalisation of capitalism
- Corporate consolidation
- The legal and political framework of economic globalisation

towards a global (economic) village: interdependence and the transnationalisation of capitalism

It is no doubt true to say that capitalism has since its beginnings always been a world or 'global' system, in the sense that the rise of capitalism coincides with, and feeds upon, the rise of colonialism and inter-continental conquest. The markets of Europe in the sixteenth and seventeenth centuries were never in this sense merely markets for local produce, with local buyers and local sellers, but were supplemented with produce from colonies and overseas 'possessions' such as tobacco, wood and precious metals. But what is equally obvious is the degree to which, over the course of the development of the modern world, we see an ever-increasing *interdependence* between markets, producers and sellers. The 'shopper' in sixteenth-century Nottingham (where the author finds himself ...) would have been choosing goods that mostly came from the surrounding area, the odd pouch of tobacco notwithstanding. Today Nottingham's shoppers are confronted by a vast array of goods from all over the world. Indeed the part of the world least represented on the shelves of the local shops would be Nottingham itself which, like so many other areas of post-industrial England, produces very little compared with even thirty years ago when it was known for the production of bicycles, lace, and cigarettes. The hero of Alan Sillitoe's famous novel (and film) *Saturday Night and Sunday Morning*, set in the Nottingham of the 1950s, was an industrial factory worker living amongst other factory workers. Now he would be more likely to be a security guard or telesales operative. But what does this interdepend-ence actually mean? What does it mean to be increasingly interdependent apart from the fact that there is more to buy in the shops?

Thinking in terms of capital itself it becomes obvious that, over the course of the twentieth century, owners have removed capital, that is money, assets and resources from local, regional and national contexts in the pursuit of greater profit. Capitalists were once local people investing in local businesses, using local employment. This is no longer the case. Since the Second World War capital has become increasingly mobile, increasingly 'liquid', meaning that capitalists have been able to invest wherever they see the greatest possible return on their investment. They have been able to take advantage of ever-diminishing costs in terms of air-freight, communications infrastructure and IT capabilities to 'outsource' production to hitherto far-flung parts of the world. Such changes are often referred to in the specialist literature in terms of the transition from '*national* capitalism', to '*multinational* capitalism' and finally to '*transnational*' or 'global' capitalism proper. These labels give some idea of what is said to have occurred. The term 'globalisation' is more commonly used than any of these more specialist terms, but globalisation or, better, *economic globalisation* is just another term for the same phenomenon, i.e. the growing interdependence of the world economy. Again, there is nothing new about interdependence or the 'world economy', as a glance at, say, Marx's *The Communist Manifesto* or Smith's *The Wealth of Nations* reveals. It is the *degree* to which we are interdependent that is striking and particularly so over the course of the last thirty years. But what does it all amount to?

To go back to the example above, we noted that what determines the success or failure of the producer is her capacity to drive costs down to survive the intense competition that characterises the capitalist market place. Capitalists *must* do whatever they can to stay 'ahead of the game' which means being able to compete with others in the market place on price and in turn cost. As we know costs vary from place to place and from country to country. In the global North the cost of living is pretty high. Housing costs are expensive. We need a lot of heating because of our miserable winters. Thus the *basic* costs involved in producing anything are themselves relatively high, not least because of the high cost of keeping a worker working. By contrast, when I visited Indonesia recently I was told that the cost of living since the 1997 Asian economic crisis, had gone back in some areas to the price of a bowl of rice per day per person. No need for housing or heat: people could 'sleep out' in that lovely climate of theirs. Certainly the costs are low compared with the cost of living in the UK or US. Back in 1945 Indonesia was a far-off country that not many people knew much about, but by 1980 plenty knew all about it – and those neighbouring countries which shared its 'low cost' attributes.

Now from the point of view of *intense competition* it is simply 'irrational' for capitalists not to take advantage of ('exploit') those conditions which aid the reduction of their costs. Why? Because if I can lower costs then *not* to do so will be to leave myself open to the possibility that someone else *will*, in turn putting me out of business. Being the 'rational' people they are, what we see over the course of the latter third of the twentieth century is capitalists engaging in a wholesale transfer of production from relatively expensive economies in the global North to relatively cheap economies in the global South. Where did all those industries in Nottingham go? One barely needs to ask the question. I once owned a Raleigh bike which would have been manufactured here in the city. Raleigh bikes now boast that they are 'made in Vietnam', hardly a fact a company would want to boast about twenty years ago. This, in microcosm, is the story of the last thirty years and, in turn, the story of the 'trans-nationalisation of capitalism'. The British owners of Raleigh bikes looked around to see where the cheapest places were to install them-selves, and off they went. As Allan Spencer, operations director for Raleigh put it in an interview with the BBC, 'The decision to close the factory doesn't reflect on the workers – it is a question of global economics and economy of scale and other factors' (as reported: www.news.bbc.co.uk/1/hi/england/2519053.stm). So farewell Nottingham! Nice to have known you for 120 years! It (almost) goes without saying that what goes for Raleigh, goes for virtually every major company involved in manufacturing in the advanced industrial world.

So over the latter decades of the twentieth century capitalism became progressively *internationalised*, meaning that more and more production circled around the globe looking for the cheapest places to set up. Volkswagen went to Czechoslovakia, Spain, Poland; Ralph Lauren to Indonesia (nice climate); Raleigh bikes to Thailand and Vietnam, and the really big corporations like Coca-Cola, Nike, Ford, Shell, McDonald's and Citibank just went anywhere and every-where they could. This is what 'transnational' as opposed to 'multi-national' means. Multi-national corporations can be found in a number of countries; transnational corporations are by contrast ubiquitous. The concept of bounded locale as in 'national' is simply meaningless for them. They are *all over the place*. Thus the constraint of operating under local, regional, or national contexts in order to drive down costs has given way dramatically under the need to com-pete more effectively, which in turn leads to greater profit, and in turn to greater investment. All this is because it is (remember) in capital's *own* interest to seek the cheapest possible cost base, the cheapest resources and labour that it can find to produce the goods it wishes to produce. Such developments conform to what we might term the 'logic of capitalist accumulation'. This is to say that to keep her business going the capitalist entrepreneur has to compete effectively, and this in turn means finding the most productive, most competitive, most commodious environment in which to operate. Not to do so is, as the history of contemporary capitalism painfully illustrates, to consign one's business to the dustbin of history. It was for this reason that even Marx argued there is little point in blaming *individual* capitalists for the character of capitalism. They are busy 'outsourcing', 'streamlining', 'down-shifting', 'flexibilising' because under a competitive market order they need to do whatever it is permitted to do to compete effectively. It is march or die.

corporate consolidation: the big just got bigger

We noted earlier, however, that in order to succeed in the market place you can either reduce your costs further than your competitors or you reduce the number of competitors through merger, incorporation or 'take overs'. As we further noted, such developments send shudders down the spines of *both* pro- *and* anticapitalists for fear of the creation of monopolies. Nonetheless *corporate consolidation* is a key part of the story of contemporary capitalism and helps explain why it has the character it has, and indeed why it is that the energies of so many anti-capitalists have been directed at 'corporate power'. The degree of consolidations is indeed striking, particularly as regards older, capital intensive industries such as car manufacturing, shipbuilding or steel making. To take cars as an example: in the immediate post-war period there were literally hundreds of manufacturers in Europe. Now one can count them on the fingers of two hands – one if we count the indigenous major players like Fiat and Volkswagen. On my embarking on the writing of this chapter, it was reported that Matra, the last of the small French manufacturers has been collapsed into Renault. The Matra 'brand' *may* be preserved if Renault can find a use for it. If it cannot, then it is farewell to Matra too. But it is not just these traditional industries that have experienced accelerating consolidation. Look around the world of the media, luxury goods, software, drinks companies, banking. Everywhere one looks the story is the same: merger, acquisition, strip down, 'streamlining'.

The survival of a multitude of brands in our shops does not, confusingly, obviate the point. Between them Unilever and Proctor and Gamble own hundreds of brands of soap powder, detergents, dishwasher tablets and so forth. The fact that the shelves of our supermarkets groan under the weight of an astonishing range of products should not be taken as a sign that there is an astonishing array of competitors out there in the market place for household products such as these. There *was* an astonishing range of competitors, but they became gobbled up by the 'big two' as part of their efforts to shape the market place in accordance with their own interests. Again, it seems we will be wasting valuable energy blaming individual companies for looking after their own interests in ways which are legal and part of 'the game'. If there is a fault to be found in this scenario then it lies with the rules of the game, or rather with those who invent and maintain 'the rules of the game'.

Here, however, matters get more complicated because the gap between the 'players' and the 'makers of the rules' has narrowed markedly to the point where we begin to see that often the 'players' and the 'makers' are the same people, albeit with different 'hats' on. In the case of large corporations such as Unilever, they not only make soap powders, they also 'help' make the rules by which international commerce is regulated (or not). As Michael Moore, George Monbiot and Gregory Palast (amongst the many) have documented, large corporations 'help' by buying the favour of the political elites. They fund election campaigns, commercials for local politicians, holidays for politicians, school fees, medical fees, and lots of other 'useful' services besides. They like things as they are, and they are prepared to do a *lot* and spend a *lot* to make sure that they remain so. This too is part of the 'game' of contemporary capitalism.

the legal and political framework

Reflecting this latter point, one of the characteristics of contemporary capitalism is that it takes place within a *legal and political framework* that is now, reflecting the internationalisation of trade itself, 'global' in scope. Here we need to mention those various agencies and institutions set up by the most powerful states after the War to oversee the development of international trade. Their aim was to prevent the kind of economic instability seen in the inter-war period, one that fatally undermined democracy in Germany and led to a severe crisis of confidence in the capitalist world more generally. The names of the institutions will be familiar to most people reading this book, as their various meetings tend to provide the pretext for anti-capitalist carnivals and protests, as for example at Seattle, Prague, Quebec City and Genoa. These institutions include the *International Monetary Fund* (IMF), The *G8*, the *World Bank*, and the *Organisation for Economic Cooperation and Development* (OECD). We need to mention too the various agencies of the United Nations involved in economic or socio-economic regulation, particularly the *United Nations Conference on Trade and Development* (UNCTAD). The *World Trade Organisation* (WTO) was set up much later in 1995 to provide a permanent institutional focus for the *General Agreement on Trade and Tariff* (*GATT*) discussions which attempt to make the 'free' market even 'freer', that is free from the barriers that prevent businesses circling around in 'perfect' liberty.

What should be made clear is that it was the major capitalist states that set up these institutions, and they did so quite self-consciously to further their own *particular* interests (usually meaning nationally based economic interests), as well as the interests of capital *generally*, which is to say the interests of transnational companies like Unilever and Coca-Cola – no surprise there. Indeed it is hardly controversial to note that the rationale of these institutions is to make the life of capitalists as easy and uncomplicated as possible by facilitating the ability of capital to move freely, to compete on a 'level playing field', through currency reform, through 'opening up' markets to 'free' competition and ensuring the necessary 'flexibility' of the labour market. This is all in the name of enhancing, promoting and facilitating the ability of capitalists to make profits, which is after all *why* they are in business. Now, however, capitalists have to make their profits 'legally', that is, by abiding by the strictures of institutions they helped set up. This is by contrast with earlier centuries when elites just did whatever they wanted, making people slaves, conquering 'undiscovered' lands, utilising 'unclaimed resources'. So it sounds like an easy ride for business: they, after all, designed and operate the institutions. But, is it?

We'll learn more about this later, but just for the moment we need to return to what was just mentioned, namely the distinction to be drawn between the *particular* interests of capitalist states and the interests of 'capital' *generally*. One of the fascinating aspects of the politics of international trade is that since the creation of these institutions it is evident that the gap between the particular and the general interests of capital has never been eliminated. This is to say that since the dawn of international trade there has always been a degree of friction between the demand for 'free trade' and the desire of particular states to protect their own producers *from* free trade, usually through protectionist measures or 'tariffs'. To be clear on this key point, a tariff is a tax that one country places on imports from another, usually in order to protect 'home' producers from cheaper goods arriving from abroad.

The example of tomato growing is actually instructive here, for one of the sources of greatest friction has been between those with relatively small-scale agricultural production such as France, and those with *either* large scale agricultural production (such as the US) *or* with very cheap labour costs by comparison with the French *agriculteur* (such as the developing world). In practice this means that French (and EU) representatives lobby hard and long for protective tariffs for their agriculture, whilst at the same time bemoaning the fact that other people's markets are closed for the kind of goods that *they* produce at low cost relative to others. Similarly, expensively subsidised cotton farmers in the US lobby hard to be allowed access to the markets of the developing world, whilst the US sets limits on the in-flow of steel, which it produces at high cost relative to countries such as South Korea. This leads to the practice of what is known as 'dumping', where producers in rich states who have received a government subsidy for manufacturing a commodity gain access to markets where the same commodity is produced at 'real' cost, i.e. without subsidy. The result is, for example, that sugar produced in the EU trades for less in many of the markets of the developing world than the latter's 'home' sugar, in turn driving producers in the developing world out of business, despite the fact that in 'real' terms they produce sugar much more cheaply than EU farmers. Such tragic outcomes are a direct correlate of the developing world's lack of bargaining 'muscle' at the WTO where the detail of who can 'dump' what on whom gets decided.

The position of the US and the EU is unsurprisingly crucial in the context of the development of international trade, yet it is a position that arouses controversy amongst 'globalisation' watchers. The question that specialists in the field squabble over is this: when these two 'blocs' defend the interests of transnational corporations, do they do so from the position of wanting to defend their own *particular* interests, or from the point of view of the interests of transnational capitalist corporations, most of which are 'American' or 'European' in origin? Depending on one's answer to the question globalisation will either appear like a neo-imperial project for the benefit of the wealthy North, or it will appear to be a process in which a *genuinely* global class (sometimes called the 'transnational capitalist class' or 'global economic elite') is in the process of detaching itself and its interests from national control, *including* the control of particular nation states. To contemplate the issue of global economic power in the 'abstract' is like looking at one of those 'duck-rabbit' pictures where, depending on one's 'hardwiring', one will see either a duck or a rabbit, or both interchangeably. On the other hand, what one 'sees' does have important implications for thinking about who or what the 'agent' of global capitalism or economic globalisation is – if there is *an* agent. It is thus a key matter for anti-capitalists to resolve, as we shall see in later chapters.

Squabbling between these various interests and dimensions of capital has been the pattern for better or worse since international trade became institutionalised. Where once protectionist measures were met with bombardments or a 'shot across the bows', now they are met with the huffing and puffing of expensively kept officials meeting in luxury conference centres. Nonetheless, this notion of the legal and political context within which capitalism operates is and will be an important one for our discussion, for what it implies is that, with *changes to the rules and regulations* of international trade, capitalism can be shaped according to different needs and interests. This is a source of hope for quite a number of anti-capitalists (particularly of the 'reform' variety), as it implies that the rules and regulations of international trade can be made 'fairer', and thus aid those who find their own interests or way of life at odds with those of big business. This is particularly so in the case of the very poor countries, which historically have done worst out of this postwar trade regime, as many who have served on such bodies freely admit. Joseph Stiglitz, former Chief Economist at the World Bank, presents an alarming picture of just this kind of infra-warfare between representatives of global capitalism in his *Globalization and its Discontents*, mostly (as he notes) at the cost of the development of the 'developing' world.

At this point we can review what we think the main differences are between contemporary capitalism and older variants, i.e. those that existed before the war. Contemporary capitalism is marked by an ever-increasing interdependence, that is by *economic globalisation*. Capital is much more fluid: it 'flows' much more readily looking for the optimum conditions with which to reproduce itself and in turn accumulate greater capital. Businesses look around the *world* not just around the locale, the region or the nation for greater profit. Contemporary capitalism is marked by the rise to pre-eminence of *transnational corporations* which in terms of their size and power are able to take advantage of whatever opportunities exist to lower the costs of production, typically by shifting production from wealthier to relatively poorer countries, or through consolidation, merger or 'take-overs'. Finally, contemporary capitalism takes place within a regime of *global governance* that seeks to accommodate both the particular interests of nation-states (rich and poor) and the needs of transnational capital, which seeks access to open markets and cheaper resources. What still needs to be asked is how any of this came to be regarded as rational or worth defending. Is capitalism just for capitalists?

learning to love capitalism

On the face of it capitalism looks a bad deal for many. After all, all this talk about 'outsourcing', 'flexibility', the collapse of Raleigh, Matra etc. means that real people in real places have lost jobs, and have had to move away to find new ones. It means that villages, towns and cities that once had jobs no longer have them. It means that those sometimes intricate networks of friends, relations and associates break up and disappear. It can mean the difference, quite literally, between life and death. Economic competition is tough. So much is too obvious to bear repeating. How then can all of this be considered 'just' or 'fair' – as of course it is not just by capitalists themselves, but by many ordinary men and women?

Looking back over the history of economic and political thought and the work of those who have sought to defend capitalism, two different arguments are clearly pertinent: the argument from *liberty* (or freedom) and the argument from *utility* (or economic growth). Most liberal theorists, who in turn did the most to establish a moral or ethical basis for capitalism, considered both arguments to be important, though they did so in different measure and to different degrees. But in order to rehearse the basis of the 'neoliberal' retrenchment of the 1970s it will be useful to keep them apart.

the argument from liberty

To the early liberals the rise of capitalism or 'mercantilism' represented a great advance on hitherto existing society for reasons that
have already been touched upon. For them pre-capitalist society
meant feudal and pre-feudal forms in which most of the population
was held in some form of subjugation. Kings and nobles were free,
priests were too, but as for the rest of the population, it existed
mostly within the powerlessness and poverty that
born serfs or slaves. The emergence of capitalism
gence of the individual from the black night of a
your 'opportunities' were limited by the fact of b
conditions to be born a serf meant to die a serf, irrespective of
one's talents, capacities or worth. Under capitalist conditions, however, more of us find ourselves in a situation where our destinies are
to varying degrees contingent, and open to choices we make or don't
make. We lack a master, for one thing. Being thrust into the world
without a master was the very quality celebrated by early liberal
theorists and enshrined in the idea of the 'rights of man'. And what
are these rights? To the seventeenth-century philosopher John Locke,
they were the right to 'life, liberty and property'. We are free: free
to work for whomever we please, or not. Free to take our own
chances, to set ourselves up, to try something novel or profitable. It
is also a freedom to fail, a 'freedom' to find oneself homeless and
unemployed. Capitalism celebrates such freedom as the essence of
its own creation. Without freedom those essential constituents of
the capitalist 'space' are lost: wage labour, new ideas, innovation.
Much later the philosopher Isaiah Berlin was to call such a conception the idea of 'negative liberty'. Negative liberty expresses the
thought above. 'Freedom' is 'freedom *from*': freedom from arbitrary
interference; from other people's plans; from government meddling;
from clerics and priests; from people one has not chosen to be with.
What is thus implicit in such an understanding is that the state is fine
as long as it is protecting my freedom defined in these terms, but bad
when it goes beyond the protection of each person's rights, particularly my right to my 'justly' acquired property. As a system built on
the right of private property, capitalism conforms to, and indeed
fully embraces, this notion of freedom, as the following example will
help demonstrate.

Take the issue of salaries: who should get what? According to this
conception, what the government or the state or public opinion

thinks is irrelevant. I have a right to my property and you have a right to yours. I own a tomato business and you need a job. I offer you 10 cents a day, which you are free to accept or decline. The next year, I judge that economic conditions have worsened and thus that I should cut wages, so I offer you 5 cents a day. Meanwhile Jordan Beckham, a famous tennis player, is to be paid a million cents a day. How could this be considered unjust? According to this conception of freedom, individuals are free to earn whatever they can. If you turn down my 5 cents a day, then you have exercised your rights not to be 'exploited' on my tomato farm, but this still leaves you looking for money. Similarly, someone is prepared to pay Jordan Beckham a lot of money to play a sport, because they think he is *worth* that. Sport is big business and successful sportsmen and women can command huge fees because a lot of people want to watch them play, buy shirts with their name or posters to put on their wall. Given these huge sums, perhaps the appropriate question to ask would be: *who else* do we think should get the money from the shirts, posters, entrance tickets? Would we be happier if more money went to the 'fat cats' who own the clubs or businesses concerned?

For many liberals this is what freedom is like: some will win, and some will lose; but whether one wins or loses is not *arbitrary*. That is, it is not based on the whim of a tyrant, a king or a priest, as it was in the past. It is based on what you are worth *to others* or what others will willingly give you. So the argument from the position of liberty insists that being free is about having rights and being able to exercise those rights with the least possible interference from others. We should be allowed to get on with our own lives. If this means the world is *incredibly* unequal (as it is), then this is the price of freedom. There are only so many 'Jordan Beckhams' out there. Such individuals may be 'lucky'; they may owe their success to being incredibly athletic, or being seven foot tall, or handsome, or blessed with a good voice or huge feet (like Ian Thorpe, the Australian swimmer). An important point in this context is that what goes for individuals, goes for countries too. There is for libertarians of this hue a *direct analogy* between the relative position of individuals and the relative position of states. The US and Britain are 'lucky' countries blessed with hard-working entrepreneurial individuals, important natural resources such as petrol, good trading links, and a long history of settled institutional development. But they have *earned* their relative wealth through global trade. Other countries are not so lucky or are, in some other way, hampered from doing as well as the US or Britain.

It is for this reason that they are much poorer. They are not poor *because* the latter two are rich. Economics is not in this view a zero-sum game. If everyone plays by the rules of 'just acquisition' everyone can get what they want, what they need. They might not get it today, or tomorrow; but if they strive hard, get lucky, then *perhaps* one day they too will strike gold.

the argument from utility

Consideration of capitalism from the point of view of utility gives a quite different slant on the matter, one that is probably more recognisable as the basis most defenders of contemporary capitalism use to justify their position. The argument is again classical, being associated principally with the work of Adam Smith and J.S. Mill and, more recently, with economists such as Hayek and Milton Friedman. What these thinkers argued is that a (capitalist) market society is not only a free society (see above), it is also a *productive* society. It works, and in working it provides employment, dynamism, opportunity. What after all is competition *doing*? At the consumer end of the scale, it is bringing down prices and enlarging choices for shoppers. If you have found yourself wondering why it is that goods are getting cheaper – DVDs, digital cameras, cars, holidays, indeed bicycles and linen (for readers in Nottingham), then the answer is because of all these things we have just been discussing: competition, lowering costs, opening markets, increasing productivity due to enhanced use of technology. All that outsourcing, downsizing, flexibilising is at one level for 'us', or for us as shoppers. The capitalist is doing us a *personal* service: she wants to make a profit, and in doing so she is benefiting us, making our lives easier, cheaper, more fun, more mobile, more creative, more *whatever*. If she wasn't she would, as we know, go out of business.

Nor is the 'happiness' confined simply to the consumer end of the scale, for what a competitive market system encourages at the *producer* end is risk-taking and entrepreneurship which in turn leads to job creation, employment opportunities, and thus to personal and collective wealth. As Smith famously noted, all this happens by operation of the 'invisible hand', which is to say that it is not even an intended outcome of the acts of individual capitalists (though it may be). We are not in other words talking about virtuous activity, but activity which necessarily has virtuous *outcomes*. My desire for money, wealth, glory, self-satisfaction leads me to set up a business which in turn requires the labour of others. From such desires come opportunities and employment for *others*. Self-interest is the motor that drives economic progress and which leads to highly dynamic societies. Where self-interest is curbed by state intervention, then economic stagnation follows. Whilst East Germans putt-putted around in their lovable but ugly Trabants, their West German neighbours were zooming up and down the autobahns in BMWs and Mercedes. Why? Because the West Germans had a free market economy that encouraged entrepreneurial activity, whilst the East Germans laboured under a suffocatingly paternalistic planning state that all but outlawed similar behaviour. The result was almost complete stagnation in the East and astonishing economic dynamism over a forty year period in the West. West Germany was not a more equal society than the East. Deviation from the *mean* wage was much higher (on official figures) in the West than in the East; but since the overall standard of living was much higher in the West, even the poor were better off there with access to better public services than the 'universal' services provided in the East. Wealth is in this view a *correlate* of inequality in capitalist economies: we (paradoxically) need inequality to make us all wealthier.

So working back from the premise we can see that a society that was concerned about the well-being of its inhabitants would do all it could to provide the most welcoming environment possible in which those individuals could be encouraged to take risks, to set up new businesses, to try out new ideas and be able to rebound quickly from failure. This would be an *entrepreneurial society*, rather than a society based on *dependence* – on the state, on the tax payer, on charity, on kind people. So in this view, the justification for capitalism is that it promotes economic growth and dynamism as well as, in turn, the economic well-being of individuals, of society, and by extension the world. And to do this we need a free market, a market that is, with the fewest possible encumbrances, tariffs, taxes, obstacles to overcome, hurdles to clear, bars to jump over. We should be free to get on with it, because 'getting on with it' will in and of itself lead to greater benefits for others.

Transferring to the global debate, what we are describing is what is known by pro- and anti-globalisers as *the 'trickle down' theory of development*. Capitalists are going to get rich in a free market, but in enriching themselves they will provide opportunities, employment, goods for the rest of us. Thus some of that overall created wealth finds its way down the pyramid. But how? Remember the point made above about costs? Down there at the bottom of the pyramid people will sometimes work for as little as a bowl of rice a day. Companies come along, set up, more employment is created, other companies arrive. Labour shortages begin to kick in, so companies need either to pay a little bit more to keep their workers or move somewhere else. Now as the 'somewhere elses' come in their turn to be developed, the effect of capitalist competition is to create a virtuous circle of mutual interdependence. The logic is that countries that are poor today will be better off tomorrow through the action of free trade and capital mobility.

This is such a key point in the overall case for global trade that we need to look more closely at the issue. Let's imagine a capitalist planet (Planet Milton) with ten communities (C1–10). C1 is very rich, C10 is very poor (they live on the dark side of the planet). Because C1 is so rich, companies find they have to pay a lot to get anyone to work for them, so two apple growers head off to C2. They find they are able to grow apples very well there, labour is cheap and thus they make big profits. Other apple growers come along as well, as do cucumber growers, grass planters, and gold miners. They all find the same. It's cheap, people work hard. But as more time passes and more companies arrive from C1, the people of C2 find they have plenty of choices of where to take their labour, and the companies are now having to pay more in order to keep them. After a while the people of C2 find they have the savings to start up their own businesses, so there is even greater pressure on wages as the companies from C1 compete with the companies from C2 for available labour, which is now pretty expensive. So some of the companies from C1, and even some from C2, head off to C3 where labour is cheaper. After a while the pattern is repeated: C3 begins to look expensive, so they move off to C4, then C5. *Eventually* they make it to C10.

For C1 read the US, Britain, France; for C2 read Japan, for C10 read Burundi, Eritrea and Nepal. One day their turn will come. It's evidently not quite their turn yet, but those clever folks at the World Bank understand the *tendency* of 'trickle down', so they are confident that even the C10s of the world will have 'their day in the sun', not just literally, but metaphorically. They know that what we need is not less free trade, but *more* free trade; not less freedom, but *more* freedom. More is good.

neoliberalism and the end of the political

So what of *neoliberalism*? How do these arguments link to the current phase of development, termed by anti-capitalists, *neoliberal
globalisation*? As the name implies, *neo*liberalism is essentially a
restatement of the classical strands of liberalism we have just been
discussing. There is nothing very novel about neoliberal ideas as
such. What is novel is the sense in which they have gained a purchase
on the minds of political and economic elites across the world.
Thinking back over the previous century, what is apparent is the
degree to which these classical statements of liberty had declined
into virtual unimportance. A cursory survey of political discourse
over the period from 1929 (the period of the Wall Street Crash) to
the late 1960s and early 1970s reveals the degree to which it was
social democratic, Keynesian and welfarist arguments that held sway
in the advanced industrial countries, even in the US. The elites had
accepted – or, more realistically, had been made to accept – that part
of the task of government was to provide for citizens from 'cradle to
grave'. People needed to be housed, educated, cared for when they
were sick, given pensions, and social facilities. This is what 'progress'
meant, even more so 'progressive politics'. It was for this reason
that the tone of a work like Hayek's *The Road to Serfdom* (published
in 1944), which argued against the vogue for planning and welfare
provision, is so *shrill*. Indeed almost all of Hayek's work is infused
with a sense of *defeat*, the defeat of liberal 'orthodoxies', of
'individualism' of freedom. Libertarian liberals like himself had, he
thought, *lost* the key arguments. They had failed to stem the tide of
'collectivism' that threatened civilisation itself, Bolshevism and
Nazism being in his view mere exaggerations of the collectivist
tendencies he attacked in the nascent welfare states of Europe and
America.

All this changed with the Oil Crisis of 1973. Reacting to the US's
support for Israel in the Yom Kippur War, the major oil-producing
countries of the Middle East embargoed the West, quadrupling oil
prices and sending elites into a frenzy of recrimination concerning
the costs of economic growth, the ever-mounting burdens on business, and the suffocating cost of social democratic measures. From
here on we hear talk of the 'crisis of the welfare state', the 'overloaded
state', 'dependency culture' which were to become all too familiar as
the 1970s gave way to the 1980s. It was around this point that the

ideas we have been discussing came back with a vengeance, and were re-established as the dominant paradigm not only at national level as the conservative tide swept over the world's most 'advanced' nations, but also at global level, in the World Bank and the IMF. There is nothing like a crisis to provoke a serious rethink, and the serious rethinking was already underway. In the US Robert Nozick's *Anarchy, State and Utopia*, published in 1974, brilliantly restated the case for an ultra-minimal, ultra-libertarian politics, the rhetoric of which made its way via the think-tanks and graduate schools into what became 'Reaganomics'. In the UK Hayek became court philosopher to Keith Joseph, in turn the principal architect of 'Thatcherism'. Reaganism and Thatcherism are quite different phenomena. Whilst the former deployed the libertarian rhetoric of 'freedom' associated with Locke, the latter leaned more towards the classic liberal notions of utility associated with Mill and Smith. But the conclusions were the same: the state should do less, a *lot* less. If it did less, we would be freer and we would also benefit from the entrepreneurial forces unleashed in the wake of the 'rolling back of government'. Sounds familiar. So what did neoliberalism imply in terms of policies?

There are a number of key themes here to be itemised:

- Reassertion of the centrality of the market as resource allocator
- Substitution of supply-side for demand-side economic management
- Submission of public life and the 'commons' to commodification

Firstly, neoliberalism is most obviously a restatement of the belief in the *centrality of the market*. Sometimes this is justified by reference to liberty (people should be free to do what they want with their property), and sometimes by reference to utility (it is better in the long run if we allow people to keep more of their money as this provides an incentive to work harder). Sometimes we hear both together, as for example in the alarm in the UK and US over the salaries of corporate 'fat cats', or directors. With regard to the latter, some days we hear that it is bad for government to intervene in such matters because it is none of our business how much companies choose to pay their directors, just as it is none of our business how much a sportsman gets paid (liberty); on other days, we hear that to interfere would be to risk 'de-incentivising' directors or making British and American companies 'uncompetitive' in the global market place for 'top' people (utility).

The main thrust of the return of the market has been in terms of *privatisation* of economic activity, particularly as regards state-run or state-owned industries. This is less a factor in the US where the state had little to privatise in the first place; but in Europe and Latin America privatisation has significantly altered the balance between the private and the public sectors, 'rolling back' the decades' long process of nationalisation that was a key feature of the welfarist settlement of the middle decades of the twentieth century. Nationalised industries are 'inefficient', 'unwieldy'; they inhibit 'risk-taking' and 'entrepreneurial activity'. They had to go. But neoliberalism demands much more than competition between businesses; it also demands competition *within* businesses. Thus one of the novelties of neoliberalism is the penetration of the market into every aspect of the functioning of the enterprise, which is now itself reconstructed as a series of sub-markets. Units within the same firm compete against each other for the same work. Workers within the same firm are expected to see each other as 'resources' or competitors, encouraging the individualisation of work and, in turn, of rewards. Contrary to expectation, however, the extension of the market has itself led to massive bureaucratisation, with every 'transaction' requiring a contract and every contract requiring a tendering process, in turn necessitating an army of lawyers, accountants and consultants to pore over their ever more complex contents. Yet 'UK PLC', 'USA Inc' and 'France SA' all find themselves in thrall to the logic of 'efficiency' that the return of the market is supposed to represent.

Secondly, the neoliberal revolution implies a shift from *supply-side economic management*, as opposed to the demand-side economics that typified the Keynesian approaches of the 'post-war consensus'. Governments could no longer create demand by embarking on large scale public works which would in turn soak up unemployment, but instead had to adopt 'fiscally prudent' measures for money supply, public borrowing and the control of inflation. A low inflation economy with high unemployment is, according to neoliberal orthodoxy, better than the 'high inflation, low unemployment' economy with which it was invariably contrasted. The task of government was to create an environment in which capital could prosper; it was not to displace, moderate or 'interfere' with capital. Here the regime of global governance was also key, making governments comply with the 'austerity measures', 'structural adjustment' policies and drastic cuts to public expenditure that global elites increasingly argued were the basis for the 'stability' without which entrepreneurial activity could not take place.

Finally, we can note that the *submission of public life to the logic of the market* is intrinsic to the neoliberal argument. This is to say that for those services that remain in state hands, profit and loss accounting, the importation of managerial techniques from the private sector, and 'public-private' initiatives await. Services that remain in the public sector have to be compelled to run themselves *as if* they are private enterprises, even if they aren't. The more they act like businesses, the less they will succumb to the 'inefficiencies' and 'red tape' that dogged nationalised industries. Thus schools should be made to compete for pupils, hospitals to compete for patients, public and 'leisure' services to compete for 'customers'. The 'exceptional' character of 'public' life as opposed to the world of industry and commerce was thus seen as an old-fashioned nostrum that merely excused 'wastefulness' and 'incompetence'. Neoliberals insisted that there is no separate 'public life' outside the market, or rather there was, but there shouldn't be. There is just life; and, as we know, life is competition.

Nor does neoliberalism accept the singularity or exceptional quality of the '*commons*' – the idea that there are certain areas of life that should not and cannot be bought and sold as commodities. One of the more disturbing facets of neoliberalism has been the encouragement to regard the *whole* of life as a resource for corporate profit. In recent years, genetic patenting has illustrated the inexorable nature of the logic as companies vie to patent the very genetic building blocks of life. Some of the most vociferous demonstrations and protests of recent years have focused on the efforts of corporations such as RiceTec to patent different varieties of rice so that peasants in the developing world are forced to buy their stocks from the company. All this is not merely acceptable on a neoliberal view: it is intrinsic to it. On a neoliberal understanding there is no 'commons'; there is no outside of the 'commodity' and thus no reason why the genetic code for rice, wheat or bananas could not be bought and sold. That this is the road to the further impoverishment of the developing world whose citizens cannot afford to insulate themselves from monopolistic practices is perhaps a matter for regret, but not for *intervention*. Adam Smith would be rolling in his grave.

Whilst neoliberalism is an intellectually complex phenomenon involving diverse strands of argument, its 'beauty' (everything is relative) is that it offers a pristinely *simple* politics. Indeed it offers a simplification of the political to the extent that 'politics' ceases to have any meaning beyond terms prescribed by the market. There is little violence to the memory of the authors of the project to assert that neoliberalism represents the *end* of the political and that, moreover, this is regarded as its chief *virtue* as a doctrine. There is no 'politics' as such in Nozick's conception of utopia, and very little in Hayek's stripped down vision of a Singaporean 'post-democratic' state. Friedman thought politics was just a form of 'protectionism' for over-bloated and self-serving officialdom looking for a reason why they should be paid. 'Politics' in this view is a complicating encumbrance requiring 'judgements' of a value-laden nature and thus of an arbitrary nature. To neoliberals, there is only one rational way of measuring value, and that is in the market-place. Any answer that departs from the formula 'whatever he/she/it is worth in the market' *has* to be arbitrary, that is, based on a bureaucrat's notion of what something is worth. Politics is the Thing that capitalism could supplant if only the market – not kings, priests or bureaucrats – was allowed to hold sway. But even under the onslaught of the neoliberal revolution that swept the world in the 1980s and 1990s, politics did not go away or 'end'. It went underground.

resources

read on

Isaiah Berlin, *Four Essays on Liberty* (Oxford: Oxford Paperbacks, 1969).

Noam Chomsky, *Profit over People: Neoliberalism and Global Order* (New York: Seven Stories Press, 1998).

Wayne Ellwood, *The No Nonsense Guide to Globalization* (London and New York: Verso, 2001).

Milton Friedman, *Capitalism and Freedom* (Chicago: UCP, 2002 [1962]).

Thomas Friedman, *The Lexus and the Olive Tree* (New York: Anchor, 2000).

Friedrich von Hayek, *The Road to Serfdom* (London and New York: Routledge, 2001 [1944]).

David Held and Anthony McGrew, *Globalization/Anti-Globalization* (Oxford and Malden MA: Polity, 2002).

Eric Hobsbawn, *Age of Extremes: The Short Twentieth Century* (London: Abacus, 1994).

John Locke, *Two Treatises of Government*, various editions [1689]. Full text available online at: www.history.hanover.edu/early/locke/j-l2-001.htm

Karl Marx and Friedrich Engels, *The Communist Manifesto* [1848], various editions. Full text available online at: www.marxists.org/archive/marx/works/1848/communist-manifesto/

Robert Nozick, *Anarchy, State and Utopia* (London and New York: Blackwells, 1978).

Ayn Rand, *Capitalism: The Unknown Ideal* (New York: Signet, 1986 [1966]).

Judith Sklair, *Globalization: Capitalism and its Alternatives* (Oxford and New York: OUP, 2002).

Adam Smith, *The Wealth of Nations*, 2 vols [1776], various editions. Full text available online at: www.econlib.org/library/Smith/smWN.html

Joseph Stiglitz, *Globalization and its Discontents* (London: Penguin, 2002).

Paul Treanor, 'Neoliberalism: Origins, Theory, Definition', www.inter.nl.net/users/Paul.Treanor/neoliberalism.html

link to

www.capitalism.org
www.zmag.org
www.wto.org
www.worldbank.org
www.oecd.org
www.unctad.org

why 'seattle'?

1968, the 'end of history' and the birth of contemporary anti-capitalism

In a brilliantly polemical essay published in 1989 entitled 'The End of History?' Francis Fukuyama suggested that with the fall of the Berlin Wall history had in some important sense come to an 'end'. What he meant was not that history as 'the passing of time' had ceased or that important events would somehow be prevented from happening. What he wanted to suggest was rather that Hegel's notion of history as having an end or goal was about to be vindicated in *political* terms. Fukuyama saw something that many others were to comment upon, which is that, with the fall of the last great ideological crusade, communism, there was now a more or less tacit consensus that liberal-democracy was the 'best' or 'most desirable' political system. Liberal-democracy had emerged victorious from the Cold War, indeed, from the more fundamental clash of ideologies that characterised the post-Enlightenment world. Ideological conflict was a thing of the past. We were all liberal-democrats now. Then in the winter of 1999 came the 'battle of Seattle'. In one week – if not in one day – the appearance of 'consensus' concerning the ends and goals of 'western civilisation' disappeared in a great clamour of dissensus, of protest, of confrontation between the forces of 'liberal-democracy' and the forces of an as yet unnamed some-Thing that was most certainly *not* liberal-democratic. Part of understanding anti-capitalism is understanding how it came about, and indeed how its coming about seemed to defy the predictions of commentators such as Fukuyama. Where, it needs to be asked, did 'Seattle' come from, and why did it take the form it did?

Trying to account for a phenomenon as complex and varied as the global anti-capitalist movement will inevitably involve a simplification of complex social forces and currents. Nonetheless the impatient beginner will want to know *something* of those forces and currents, even if we can only approximate the manner in which they interact and flow into each other. Here Fukuyama can be of service,

SEATTLE – WHAT HAPPENED?

As we noted in the introduction, many commentators, both activist and non-activist, regard the Seattle protests of December 1999 as the 'moment' when the contemporary anti-capitalist/anti-globalisation movement was born. Why? On the face of it, Seattle was just like many other protests in recent years. A meeting of the WTO provided the pretext for a mass demonstration – but such protests have been regular events since the Rio Earth Summit of 1992. What was different about Seattle was, firstly, the *diversity* of groups present, and also the presence of trade unions which had been signally absent from the major protests particularly in North America up to this point. 'Teamsters' or union activists met with the 'Turtles' or environmental activists in a great activist melting pot. Secondly, there was the *nature* of the protest. The authorities in Seattle were determined not to be shown up as 'weak' in the face of a major protest involving up to 70,000 people, and thus deployed a heavy-handed approach to policing. This in turn led to violent confrontations, the use of teargas and baton rounds, in turn providing dramatic heavily mediatised images that seemed to signal the radicalisation of activism. The *effect* of the policing was in fact to promote greater solidarity between different groups which might otherwise never have spoken to each other. Debates and discussions were staged, alliances forged, networks created. Perhaps most dramatically of all, the protests actually succeeded in shutting down the meeting of the WTO thereby giving the impression that large scale mass action could achieve something more than a temporary discomfort to global elites. They could disrupt 'global capitalism' in some very tangible manner. 'Seattle' thus promoted the notion that large demonstrations were an important and immediate way in which neoliberalism could be combated.

because what he offers is an account of why it is that a radical counter-consensual current like anti-capitalism was in effect *unthinkable*. By simple deduction we can infer that if the outcome of his prediction was wrong, then elements of the reasoning must have been wrong. Looking closely at the contention he offered, we can point to two key assumptions that Seattle was finally to explode:

1. that liberal-democracy had the capacity to manage the effects of the processes outlined in the last chapter, particularly the transformation of capitalism from being essentially national in character, to being transnational or 'global'; and
2. that an oppositional *politics* necessarily stems from an oppositional *ideology*, and thus that with the 'death of communism' – if not the death of ideology as such – *oppositional* politics would wither.

With regard to 1., what becomes obvious with hindsight is, paradoxically, that the qualities celebrated in liberal-democracy by thinkers such as Fukuyama are those most under threat by these macro-economic developments. Indeed, it is little exaggeration to say that if anything triumphed in 1989 it was not 'liberal-democracy' but global capitalism. This is to say that it was not politics that triumphed over economics, as implied in Fukuyama's analysis. It was a case of *economics triumphing over the political*. Thus it might be argued that the anti-capitalist 'battle of Seattle' represented 'a return of the political', a return of ethics, morality and values in place of the vacuum created by the 'departure' of politics from the global scene. This sounds more like a conclusion than a premise, so let's take two steps back and attempt to unpack these arguments. This will help us to get a sense of the broader significance of the emergence of an anti-capitalist movement post-Seattle and will in turn help us to see what potential lies within it for the recuperation of politics itself.

problems of liberal-democracy

As a sometime teacher of Soviet politics, I used occasionally to refer to a journal entitled *Problems of Communism*. The agenda of the journal was contained in its title. Communism had of necessity 'problems' that it was the journal's task to analyse. There is no equivalent journal of liberal-democracy, which is not to say that liberal-democracy is not without its problems, because the problems of liberal-democracy are not (yet) held by mainstream political scientists to be fundamental or intrinsic to its very operation, as were communism's 'problems'. Yet, as should be clear from the discussion of neoliberalism in the previous chapter, developments over the past thirty years necessitate a reappraisal of this position. Indeed it is hardly hyperbole to suggest that the presuppositions informing liberal-democratic theory are now threatened with redundancy and need to be rethought. Why is this?

Firstly, it is evident that we are witnessing *a crisis of liberal-democratic politics.* The emergence of a *global* anti-capitalist movement is a symptom of that crisis. In particular it is a sign that not enough is being done at the national level to convince concerned individuals that political actors are capable of influencing, let alone controlling, economic actors. This is not the same as saying that the *nation-state* itself is in crisis, which is implied in much of the commentary on globalisation. Unlike their territorial forebears, the empires of the late nineteenth century, nation-states are *not* in danger of disappearing. Clearly, states are key actors internationally and will remain so for some time to come. Rather, nation-states are all too often taken hostage by forces, principally transnational corporations that are able to apply considerable pressure to ensure that their every whim is catered for. This undermines and weakens the 'sense' that politics has at the nation-state level. For 'politics' to be effective and relevant it has to be able to shape or affect the behaviour of the economic actors who do so much to shape the character and prospects of modern societies. 'Justice' is what we as a political community say is 'just', and what we say is 'just' must in turn be able to be translated into 'just' policies. Problems begin when the community has little or no control over its own affairs, when it is unable to govern itself in accordance with its own wishes. Liberal-democratic thinkers like to describe liberal-democratic politics as, in essence, one of self-government. 'We' (or rather our representatives) 'govern', and the state as the executor of our decisions carries out whatever it is we want it to do. Liberal-democratic states are *described* as governing themselves ('government of the people, by the people, for the people'). The *reality* is rather different. What happened?

Recall the last chapter: one of the most important developments of the last third of the twentieth century is the transformation of capitalism from being largely national in character, to being multi-national and then transnational or *global* in character. Much of what we term capitalism, particularly the capitalism of the major corporations is conducted beyond or outside the direct control or influence of the nation-state. Indeed the major corporations conduct themselves in a 'state-like' manner (if not a 'statesman-like' manner), acting upon their *own* self-interest as opposed to the interests of the nation associated with the company or brand. In 2002, when US giant Ford chose to announce 35,000 job cuts as part of a plan to become 'competitive', it of course 'consulted' politicians. That is it told them it was cutting jobs; but it was Ford that decided how and where the jobs were to be cut. One thousand of those jobs were to be lost from its truck assembling facilities at Edison, New Jersey. The fact that Edison is to be left devastated by the loss of key skills and workers is something that politicians, both local and national, can regret, but do little about. All they can do is attempt to smooth the transition from industrial (indeed 'Fordist') past to a 'post-industrial' future, with the creation of heritage sites, call centres and low grade supermarket work. One difficulty in terms of the problematic being discussed here is very evidently that the process propelling us towards *economic* globalisation has not hitherto been matched by a process of *political* globalisation, leaving a marked 'democratic deficit' between the two spheres. This is in contrast with the way that the process of the construction of *national* capitalism was matched – and in cases like France, *preceded* – by the construction of a *national state* implying that the activities of economic actors could, at least in theory, be shaped or determined in accordance with political priorities, as well as economic ones. Here we need to make two further observations.

Firstly, it is true as we pointed out in the last chapter that global capitalism is subject to a legal and political framework; but this framework does not of itself constitute a 'state' as that term would usually be understood, that is as a 'sovereign' coercive power with the capacity to act independently of the particular interests within. The institutions of global governance are at present subject to corporate needs and interests rather than the other way round. Whether they might be so constituted as to act like a state is a matter of heated debate within anti-globalisation circles for reasons that will become more apparent in the next chapter. Secondly, those political bodies that *do* claim quasi-sovereign character, such as the UN, are without the means of controlling the activities of global economic actors, let alone those states who choose to ignore the decisions of the UN unless it suits them to do otherwise, such as the US and

Israel. As the diplomatic run-up to Gulf War II showed, the UN is in any case only at best a quasi-sovereign body, and even this status has now to be considered as one dependent on the indulgence of the US. The net result is that whilst the domain of political authority has remained at the nation-state level, the domain of economic activity has increasingly shifted to the global level. There is *no global state* and there is no effective mechanism of *accountability* for those actors that operate at the global level, such as global corporations. The latter exist in a sort of postmodern state of nature directly accountable to no one but themselves and the shareholders of the company.

Such a situation implies that the economic domain has become ever more detached from political control and thus that the relevance of the state as a primary site for democratic decision-making is becoming diminished by the day. It is this observation that underpins the '*death of the nation-state*' thesis which has been so vigorously debated by political scientists and commentators since the late 1980s, i.e. just at the moment when Fukuyama wrote so glowingly of the 'triumph' of liberal-democracy. Now, whether or not the nation-state really is 'dead' need not detain us for long (it isn't), beyond noting that the debate is usually framed in terms of the *degree* to which the state can be said to be becoming irrelevant, not on the more general thesis that the state is 'losing power' vis-à-vis economic actors, and indeed vis-à-vis supra-national institutions such as the EU or NAFTA. For our purposes the more salient point is that the process by which capital became transnational created a political vacuum which is felt today in a number of ways that can help explain the emergence of a global anti-capitalist movement. These might be summarised as: the *decline of ideological difference* and the *decline in democratic participation*. It is 'official' politics that has borne the brunt of the vacuum created by the 'hollowing out' of the state.

the end of ideology (revisited)

Firstly, what is evident is that the *ideological differences* between political parties and thus between governing elites has diminished to the extent that many wonder what the point of 'party politics' is. This is not to say that the ideological divisions between the parties were in the past more significant than their similarities, as is sometimes implied in the commentary. As has long been noted, the tendency of electoral politics is to reduce ideological difference in an attempt to capture the centre-ground where the 'average' voter can be found. Thus it might be considered 'normal' for ideological differences to be ironed out over the long term in response to the 'need' to broaden the appeal of a party for electoral purposes. Nonetheless, it is important in terms of the *self-image* of liberal-democratic politics that voters perceive that there is a significant difference between parties, and thus that there be some element of choice as between different visions of how the country should be governed. Commentators have long remarked on the basic similarity in ideas between the Republican Party and the Democrat Party in the US; but those same commentators have often smugly noted the much deeper ideological cleavages apparent in European politics. As regards the US, the Republicans and Democrats have long traded on their 'different' concerns and values, the former standing up for entrepreneurial dynamism, the centrality of family and community, and a muscular view of America's place in the world. The latter, by contrast, championed the poor, those from ethnic or racial minorities, and those otherwise overlooked in the individualistic pursuit of the 'dream'. Yet such differences are now less significant than the similarities between the two – particularly when in power. Both parties are at their very core pro-business, pro-market, pro-individualism.

In the UK the Labour Party was seen as the champion of the working class and of social democratic or welfarist policies. Now the Labour Party, or more properly, 'New Labour', is the party of privatisation, 'private finance initiatives' and the private funding of hospitals, schools and roads. In this sense the coming to power of New Labour in 1997 hardly represented a break with the Conservatives, the party that introduced a neoliberal agenda. Indeed, many of the more controversial policies brought in by the latter were not merely endorsed, but driven on by the new administration, as for example in the case of the privatisation of the railways, reform of the health service and the introduction of tuition fees in higher education. This in turn fuels the *perception* that there is little to choose between Labour and Conservative, and thus the growing redundancy of party politics itself.

What goes for Britain equally goes for many other advanced industrial countries such as France, Australia and Germany. Around the world ideological cleavage has given way to the neoliberal orthodoxy described in the previous chapter, one built around the 'necessity' for low inflation, flexible labour markets, balanced budgets, privatisation and competition in all areas of 'public' activity. This situation is a reflection of the dominance of corporate interests that demand such conditions in return for the internal investment that brings jobs, wealth, and 'opportunity'. This is presented less as the result of a contest between unequal parties, namely the nation-state and global corporations, and more as the result of the 'prudent' and 'realistic' assessment of national interests by our representatives. In this sense the much vaunted 'Third Way' of Tony Blair, Bill Clinton and Gerhard Schroeder that called for flexible labour markets, reduced state 'interference' and the opening up of the public sector to market forces, was in essence little more than an *ex post facto* justification for a state of affairs over which they as *national* politicians have increasingly little control. To quote Mrs Thatcher once more, at the national level 'There Is No Alternative' (handily abbreviated to 'TINA'). It is 'play ball', or see the ball disappear off to some other part of the world where they better understand how 'the game' works. The Third Way gave the *appearance* of political control over economic conditions; but the *reality* is rather different. Those who wish to avoid confrontation with global economic forces are increasingly required to conform to its 'logic' even if this means abandoning the social democratic and welfarist 'consensus' they were arguably elected to protect.

anyone for voting?

As ideological cleavages have diminished (or are perceived to have diminished) so we have seen, secondly, a *decline in political participation* at the official or national level. This means a decline in voting, party membership and a more general but equally discernable decline in interest in national, supra-national *and* sub-national or local politics. Recent voting statistics in the UK as elsewhere make for gruesome reading for those concerned about the legitimacy of electoral politics, with turnouts heading below the 30% and even the 20% mark for local elections and elections to the European parliament. As regards the latter, at the 1999 European elections one constituency in the UK (Liverpool, Riverside) saw only 10% of eligible voters turn out. This is to say that *nine out of ten* voters failed to show up at all, prompting the question, at what point does the democratic 'mandate' cease to be effective? In the US the Presidential election attracts just half of all eligible voters. At Congressional level the weariness of the electorate is even more impressive, with turnouts on a par with those recorded for European elections in the UK – to say nothing about elections at state and county level, which barely register a flicker on the radar of the electorate.

In similar vein, the memberships of all major parties in the UK are in free-fall, precipitating a financial crisis, in turn pushing them further towards corporate sponsorship. The Conservatives boasted over 2 million members in the 1960s; now it has in the order of 300,000 members. Membership of the Labour party has virtually halved since its triumphant 'landslide' in the 1997 general election and is still falling. Meanwhile political coverage in the media is being continuously remodelled to appeal to 'youth'; but it seems that 'youth' has got better things to do with itself than listen to the old and wise telling them how important it is to participate in 'official' politics. Similar phenomena are well-documented across the western world and point to the decline in the perceived importance of the nation-state as the site of political contestation. Whoever we vote for, 'they' always win.

The net result is not the triumph of liberal-democracy, but the *crisis of liberal-democracy* confronted with economic forces that are largely beyond the reach or control of national governments. For our purposes this translates into a crisis of 'official' politics, that is, the politics of political parties, of elections and participation in the mainstream political process, compelling those who really *are* concerned about the state of the world into more 'unofficial' or subterranean forms of engagement. Who are these people? As implied in the comments above, we need to think here in *horizontal* terms, that is in terms of *ideological affiliation* along the spectrum of political beliefs; and also in *vertical* terms, or in terms of the 'reach' of politics from the global level down through the supra-national, then national and sub-national levels.

If the tendency of electoral politics is to push the main parties towards the centre, then this leaves 'behind' a significant number of participants who are alienated by the spectacle of the land grab at the 'middle', and thus of the necessary watering down of political demands to seek the acceptability of the party in question. This is a phenomenon that affects both the left and right of the political spectrum. Indeed, one of the tendencies of contemporary politics is the seeking of alternative outlets for both radical leftists *and* radical rightists, sometimes with perverse results. In the French Presidential election of 2002 the Marxist – or quasi-Marxist – left polled almost 15% of the national vote, taking votes from the *Parti Socialiste* (PS) and paving the way for the success of Jean-Marie Le Pen and the extreme right *Front Nationale* in the first round. In the US presidential election of 2000 many liberals and leftists backed Ralph Nader 'taking votes' from Al Gore, and (according to some) ensuring that George Bush was returned as President despite securing fewer votes than the latter. There are also the 'missing voters' who have either given up 'politics' altogether or moved 'underground', choosing to dispense with electoral politics in favour of campaigning and direct action. So the *perception* of ideological consensus around neoliberal policies has served to jolt people out of the regular political 'habits' that liberal-democratic theorists regard as key to the legitimation of the political process. Increasingly, radicals have chosen to abandon the fight *within* official political parties for control over the ideological agenda and prefer to form their own groups outside the political mainstream.

On the *vertical* plane, that is the plane between the global level of politics at one end and the local at the other, we see an analogous process taking place. This is to say, that the perceived inability of political parties and other official actors to influence or shape 'politics' at the global level encourages concerned individuals to seek 'unofficial' means for pursuing their ends. Those particularly animated by the issue of global justice and the inequalities between the Global North and the Global South have found it increasingly futile to pursue these concerns through political parties whose rationale is, traditionally, to preserve and enhance the interests of a given *national* territory. On these terms it has become much more relevant (and much more rewarding) to join one of the proliferating 'unofficial' or DIY ('do it yourself') groups whose mission is to remind the global wealthy of their obligations to the poor and indebted. In short, the vacuum we noted above with regard to the absence of global political bodies with the clout and presence to bring global economic actors to account could only be met through *unofficial* political action. How better to advance those claims than to turn up at the meetings of the WTO, the World Bank or the G8 and seek redress directly, immediately, *now*?

The same can be said for politics at the local or community level. 'Official' local politics may be in crisis, but the vacuum created has permitted a range of 'independent' voices to be heard in elections, as well as a range of community level initiatives to be unleashed. Such initiatives are not merely outside the mainstream, but they challenge it in very direct terms. The evident vibrancy of women's

groups, environmental activism, local protests at the closures of
hospitals, schools and local services, road-building and housing
projects all underline the degree to which the crisis of official politics
marks the growing importance of a different kind of politics: a disaggregated, diverse, plurality of disparate 'actions'. Politics *in this sense*
is alive and well. It has simply moved off the official political 'stage'.
Such a politics will remain subterranean and 'invisible' to elites and
the metropolitan media. Until it erupts.

1968 and the 'crisis' of oppositional politics

The above point underlines a further difficulty of Fukuyama's
confident analysis. This is the assumption that a meaningful
oppositional politics is one that has to be framed in terms of an
official ideology of 'opposition', in this case communism or Soviet
Marxism. Shared by the global elite, Fukuyama's assumption was
that the defeat of communism would provide a de facto basis for a
new consensus on the desirability of liberal-democracy, and indeed
of capitalism. And it is easy to see why they might have been lulled
into thinking in such reductive terms even when, as is now obvious,
the defeat of communism was actually a key factor permitting the
emergence of an anti-capitalist movement. If this sounds paradoxical
then we need to note that the Cold War made for a very simplified
politics. The world was divided by an elite-driven discourse into two
camps: those who defended 'freedom', or capitalism (the two being
the same in elite Cold War-speak), and those who did not. The latter
were 'communists' who had to be confronted and defeated in order
to 'protect freedom'. This simplification of politics served an
essential function for both the US and the Communist Bloc. It
allowed the former to demonise oppositional politics as 'communist'
and thus to tar oppositionists with the brush of being traitors to the
cause of freedom more generally. On the other side of the fence it
gave legitimacy to the communists' claim to be fighting on behalf of
the world's poor and oppressed. It thus annexed oppositional
activity to the interests of the Soviet Union in particular. There was
nothing like a 'third space', a space 'in-between' these blocs, creating
countless dilemmas for progressives and political radicals until the
collapse of the Soviet Union. The example of the peace movement is
instructive in this respect.

Most 'peaceniks' of the 1970s and 1980s were proudly unaligned, which is to say that what they cared about was not the interests of one or other bloc, but the need for a reduction – and preferably an elimination – of nuclear weapons and the demilitarisation of the 'front line' in Europe. The problem for such figures is that it was very much in the Soviet Union's interests to undermine support in the West for nuclear weapons. It is thus hardly surprising that the Soviets did everything they could to promote and fund the peace movement, hosting 'peace' conferences in Moscow, funding journals and movements, facilitating 'exchanges' and so forth. This in turn fell straight into the hands of those in the West who wanted to claim that the peaceniks were agents of communism, and thus had to be monitored, controlled and more generally combated in whatever ways possible. It was not easy being an oppositionist, even if 'all' one cared about was global peace.

What this global picture hid was in fact more important than what it 'revealed'. What had become evident much earlier than 1989 was that the Soviet Union's claim to represent the cause of 'anti-capitalism' was essentially bogus. Considered in terms of the prospects of the development of an oppositional politics in the West, it is clear that the 'Soviet road' was widely, if not universally, recognised as a dead-end after 1968. Indeed it was, more generally, the astonishing events of 1968 that showed the direction in which any anti-capitalist resistance was likely to go. Here we can touch upon three developments of significance for thinking about the contemporary anti-capitalist movement:

1. the final loss of credibility of the Soviet Union itself as the official agent of anti-capitalism;
2. the significance of the Paris *Évènements* as a challenge to the official Marxist-Leninist narrative of 'liberation'; and
3. the displacement of an official oppositional politics by the proliferating *unofficial* politics of 'new social movements' and special interest groups.

the prague spring and the 'end' of soviet marxism

To begin with the *position of the Soviet Union*, 1968 was the year of the Prague Spring when the efforts of the reform minded leadership of Czechoslovakia were brutally crushed by Soviet intervention. Alexander Dubcek had under pressure from 'people power' intro-duced a series of reforms dubbed 'socialism with a human face', which eased considerably the otherwise stifling rule of the Communist Party. Fearing that such measures – including greater freedom of speech and the granting of certain minority rights – would quickly lead to the demand for similar policies in the rest of the Communist Bloc, the Soviets ordered their allies in the region to join in an armed intervention to overturn Dubcek's regime. The hardliner Gustav Husak was installed and he rapidly overturned the liberal reforms. This was not of course the first such intervention to snuff out the challenge of reformism. The most hideous of them all occurred in Hungary in 1956 where Imre Nagy had attempted to introduce a liberalisation of the Stalinist measures of forebears such as Mátyas Rakosi. But the crushing of the Prague Spring had a very particular resonance for much of the Western Left. It was the final collapse of the now vain idea that the Soviet Union could be a force for good in the world; that somehow it represented the hope for a better world. The Soviet Union was finally revealed as just another form of brutal elite rule that had to be opposed by anyone wanting to develop progressive alternatives to capitalism, as opposed to the particularly reductive notion of 'socialism' on offer in the eastern bloc.

The Prague Spring had a profound effect on the more thoughtful elements of the Western Left, convincing many of them that their own interests were at odds with Great Power politics generally. The suspension of debate concerning the aims and goals of socialism in favour of the quietistic acceptance of the Soviet Union's 'leading role', so prevalent among radical intellectuals in the earlier decades of the twentieth century, gave way to a new experimentalism and a desire to re-examine the terms and conditions of their radical com-mitments. This in turn led to a profusion of socialisms and socialist groups, each with its own idea of how the world should look, how it was to be brought about, and what structures were needed to ensure participation. Even the communist movement itself, hitherto silent on the question of the Soviet Union's credibility as a 'progressive' force, fractured into various official and unofficial splinters. Discounting the various Maoisms thrown up as an ultra-radical response to the crisis of communism, the most significant of these currents coalesced around the label 'Eurocommunism'. Some of the concerns and themes of this fracturing of the left in the wake of 1968 have a resonance that can be heard in contemporary debates over the future of anti-capitalism. These include:

- The idea of the '*death of the working class*' as the agent of radical change. Sociologically, western society was, according to many, becoming 'post-industrial' or post-Fordist. The old industries that created the strong ties of identity amongst the working class were dying off, to be replaced by service industries or unemployment – neither of which provided the basis for class solidarity and collective action. If radical politics had any future it was in response to the rise of 'post-materialist' values in the young and socially marginalised, both groups being prominent in the events in Paris and Prague.

- Reflecting the above, *identity* was becoming a factor in disunity. People were more ready to identify with sub-groups and sub-lifestyles rather than with larger aggregates such as 'the working class'. It was said that people now saw themselves as part of some or other 'minority'. Accordingly mobilisation could not be effected in and through conventional mechanisms, particularly via the mass party, but had to take account of the differing needs and perceptions of minority groups.

- Post-capitalist schemas could only work on the basis of the acceptance of plurality and diversity. This led to much fashionable talk of the need to recognise the necessity for 'civil society', human rights and the opening of the sphere of democracy to new groups and new forms of representation. The seizure of state power on the Bolshevik model was firmly displaced in favour of a variety of strategies including, where pertinent, electoral participation, lobbying and direct action.

In the wake of 1968 'The Left' rapidly dissipated into various currents, some radical and transformative, others much less so. The 'fracturing of the left' hardly looks helpful from the point of view of the mobilisation of people behind an ideal that could challenge and in turn supplant capitalism. Yet what it tacitly signalled was the *complexity* of thinking through the post-capitalist 'after' and thus the necessity for a generally more open, more tolerant kind of politics so that different voices, minorities and interests could be heard. In short the perceived failure of Soviet Communism opened a space for dialogue and for the appearance of a multitude of diverse, plural and, it has to be said, conflicting accounts of how post-capitalism was to be pursued. The Prague Spring was in its own way an ideological Pandora's Box, out of which sprung a variety of radicalisms, socialisms and humanisms. The 'dream'

of a communist Front uniting the Eastern Left and the Western Left
lay in tatters. The dream was in any case no more than a 'nightmare'.
Its dissipation was the necessary prelude to a fundamental reconsider-
ation of the manner by which progressive politics could be
advanced.

paris '68: unofficial politics and the new radicalism

Such developments were further underlined by the tumultuous
events in Paris that same spring. Rather like 'Seattle' itself, the shape
of French political life was radically transformed in a matter of
hours by the efforts of an initially small number of university
students led by an even smaller coterie of tutors, intellectuals and
ideological outcasts, including some of the most celebrated (or
notorious) figures of the theoretical, ideological and political
realignment that followed '68 such as Jean-François Lyotard.
Protesting against the iniquities of university funding (in particular
the closing of the Nanterre campus), the protests quickly radicalised
and generalised into an outright rejection of the French political and
cultural establishment, and even more generally into a rejection of
the materialist values and way of life that seemed to have stultified
French life. All around Paris the now familiar slogans and images of
outright rebellion could be seen: 'Be Realistic: Demand the
Impossible'; 'Choose Life'; 'It is Forbidden to Forbid'; 'Take your
Desires for Reality'. The student protests quickly descended into a
general paralysis of Parisian life as they were joined by workers at the
huge Renault plants on the outskirts of the city. For a brief moment,
something like a re-enactment of the 1871 Paris Commune seemed
possible, together with a complete breakdown of the French state.
De Gaulle and the French elites were caught completely unawares,
with the result that the strikes spread like wildfire, paralysing
French economic and political life for a matter of weeks. It seemed
for a fleeting moment that literally anything had become possible,
including the 'impossible'. However, through a combination of
political bullying and cautious trade union leadership, the crisis
passed, leaving a bitter legacy that still excites the French political
classes on both sides of the ideological divide. How though does all
of this have a bearing on the issues under review?

Paris '68 is significant for a number of reasons. The first and most obvious is that it represented the first real upsurge of 'unofficial' politics in Post-War Western Europe. What became obvious in the unfolding of the events was that the French Communist Party (PCF), hitherto the focus for 'anti-capitalist' demands in France, had become an irrelevance from the point of view both of the uprising itself, and the demands and 'politics' that it represented. The PCF seemed part of the problem not part of the solution. According to its critics, the PCF was a large, unwieldy and utterly bureaucratised 'mainstream' party that seemed content merely to act out its anointed 'role' as 'oppositional' counter-weight to the centre and right. In this sense it had become part of the political establishment, and as far distant from the concerns of the young as any other party. Its tired narrative of factory-based struggles, heroic sacrifices and command planning was by-passed by a much more anarchic, spon- taneous and free-flowing discourse of 'immediate' liberation from the suffocating weight of all inherited 'roles', whether they be based on 'class', 'ideology' or any other prepackaged formula. In this sense the dominant credo of '68 was hardly Marxist in the orthodox sense of the term at all, but more nearly 'situationist', after the Situationist International.

Formed earlier in the late 1950s by avowedly *ex*-Marxist (in the official sense) figures such as Guy Debord and Raoul Vaneigem, the Situationists offered an original mix of Sartrean existentialism, Dada-inspired surrealism and a loose-limbed variant of historical materialism that focused on the corrosive effects of the consumer society, on personal and collective autonomy. What they proposed was an essentially aesthetic 'break-out' from conformity to roles, to stereotypes, political parties, majoritarianism, and the mainstream. In their view, capitalism had to be resisted not only at the level of the 'political', of institutions and structures of power, but also at the level of the personal, of the subject of politics, of his or her *desires*. From this position emerged a novel strategy of resistance based, not upon the revolutionary seizure of power, but upon a process by which capitalism would be *subverted from within* as a prelude to its dis- placement by other ways of living. How was this to be achieved? Two themes are important for the purposes of considering the rele- vance of these ideas for contemporary anti-capitalism: the idea of the *détournement* of the capitalist 'aesthetic' and thus the capitalist structure of desire; and the idea of the 'spectacle' as a medium for eliciting resistance as well as compliance.

détournement, the 'spectacle' and contemporary anti-capitalism

Taking *détournement* first, the idea was that through a subtle juxtaposition or alteration of capitalist 'signs' we would be compelled to reflect on the authenticity of the need for whatever it was that was being offered as a satisfier of our 'desires'. This could be a simple gesture such as drawing a moustache on the image of a 'desirable' woman being used to sell perfume. This would in turn subvert the message we are supposed to glean from the ad: wearing this perfume will make one as 'glamorous' as the women in the picture. Advertising could be defaced, scribbled on, reworded, all in the name of producing a moment's reflection on the part of the observer, but reflection (so it was hoped) not just on the commodity value of the thing being sold, but on the nature of 'commodity fetishism', the manner by which objects are imbued with apparently magical, sexual or otherwise 'heightened' properties for the purpose of making them more desirable to the consumer. *Détournement* has now become a central pillar of anti-capitalist resistance the world over, though the term 'subvertising' or 'guerrilla advertising' are more familiar. *Adbusters*, the collective that produces the slickly produced journal of the same name, deploys the Situationist strategy of *détournement*, using digital techniques to mask or overcode advertising, as well as chronicling the efforts of the many groups involved in 're-facing' billboards in the US. As Naomi Klein documents in *No Logo*, subvertising is a key strategy, particularly in the US, in the war against the commodification of life, aimed at corporate power and the penetration of logos, brands and advertising into hitherto sheltered domains of existence such as schools and libraries. As is evident, 'culture jamming' is a direct inheritance of the situationist understanding of political resistance as one based on a struggle at the level of 'the everyday' for the hearts and minds of the denizens of advanced industrial society.

The same is true for the notion of the spectacle as a key plank of resistance countering the spectacle of capitalist commodification. To the Situationists, capitalism is a highly visual aesthetic: it seeks to retain our interest, make us aware of brands, logos, shopping malls, publicity, so that we will buy more. A resistance that fails to engage with capitalism in the visual and emotional field will thus fail to challenge the stranglehold it exercises over our sense of who and what we are. A fundamental disruption thus has to be effected in front of us, indeed within us. Resistance was regarded to be not just about power, about storming offices and throwing out 'the ruling class', but also about changing our view of the world both literally and metaphorically. Nor could resistance be a quietistic or theory driven exercise, but had to be a counter-spectacle, an alternative aesthetic experience. Like the concept of *détournement*, the idea of the spectacle has been taken up and accounts, at least in part, for one of the most interesting facets of anti-capitalist protests which is that of the quite self-conscious attempt to capture the feel of a carnival or circus. There is noise, music, colour, drama, costumes, theatre, giant sculpture. It could be argued that this emphasis on the aesthetic dimension of protest reaches further back still to the medieval carnivals that toured the market towns and villages of Europe. It is also suggestive of the carnivals of the peasants and landless poor across the developing world, each regarded with dread by governing elites. Nonetheless the idea of carnival as a basis for resistance in capitalist states was one of the great 'rediscoveries' of 1968 and lives on today in the strategy and outlook of key anti-capitalist groupings such as Reclaim the Streets and *Ya Basta!*

More generally, such developments portend the sense in which traditional revolutionary strategies which focused on the capturing of state power through a physical occupation of the space of 'the state' were challenged in significant ways, as too were the traditional means by which the 'masses' were to be mobilised. It was no longer enough to shout slogans through a loudhailer to effect a change in the way people thought about themselves. Nor could a mobilisation be effected through bureaucratic and unwieldy party machines. People would somehow have to divest themselves of their emotional investment in commodities, and more generally in capitalism, *in order to make* capitalism 'collapse'. They needed to *desire* radical change before radical change became a possibility. A politics that ignored the place of desire could on this reading only repeat the mistakes of earlier revolutionaries. Such a politics was of necessity 'unofficial' in scope and character. It was a politics of guerrilla tactics, of *détournement*, of aesthetic and subjective rebellion. It was, in the memorable phrase of the period, about making *oneself* a 'revolutionary of everyday life'. Such sentiments were to become increasingly prevalent in the run-up to Seattle and the emergence of the mobile carnival of resistance that was to become such a central feature of contemporary radical politics.

1968, 'new social movements' and direct action

Lest it be forgotten, 1968 was a momentous year more generally for the emergence of unofficial politics. This had two aspects: the first as a *mobilisation against war*, and the second as a *mobilisation against the exclusion of women, minorities, groups and issues* hitherto over-looked or disregarded by mainstream or 'official' politics. The Vietnam War and the Civil Rights Movement both initiated an unprecedented degree of mobilisation in the US and Europe, one with important lessons for today. Both the War and Civil Rights activism engaged and mobilised ordinary people in a manner with-out precedent in US politics, in turn serving to radicalise a gener-ation of activists. What it showed in particular was that a mass mobilisation could be effected against an injustice rather than for some ideologically delineated vision. This is to say that *injustice* could be just as effective, if not more so, in terms of uniting people and encouraging them to reflect on the nature and circumstances of the power behind the injustice. It also demonstrated the utility of *direct action* as opposed to 'official' political activity such as voting or standing for office. Direct action worked in the sense that in a televis-ual age, the image of thousands of young people protesting against lines of soldiers, placing flowers in their guns, chanting and singing for peace was an important signal that a significant element of the population would not accept the legitimacy of the War without resistance. Nor, increasingly, would people accept the sight of Afro-Americans being beaten by the police for demanding nothing more than equality with their white peers. Fear of mobilisation has since the dawn of liberal-democracy been a powerful catalyst for changing politicians' minds, particularly those concerned for their electoral prospects. There is nothing like the sight of 'mobs' and 'crowds' to concern politicians who in general much prefer the docility of elec-tions and parliamentary debate. From this point of view the mobil-isations probably were significant in the decision of the US administration to pull out of Vietnam, as it finally did in 1973. It was at least in part the experience of the anti-war movement that encouraged the growth of unofficial politics in the immediate aftermath of 1968. The most prominent such development was the development of the women's movement across the advanced indus-trial world, and in later decades across the developing world too. Ironically, the growth of the women's movement was partly in response to the negative experience of women in the anti-war protests and to shared feelings of being excluded in the unstructured decision-making that underpinned the anti-war mobilisation. Like the anti-war movement, however, the effectiveness of the movement was largely framed in terms of its being *against* something that to most progressively minded individuals was clearly unjust, namely the deep inequality and voicelessness experienced by women across the world. And again, the remedy was often various forms of direct action ranging from demonstrations and sit-ins, to the invasion of the Miss World contest and the disruption of UK parliamentary proceedings and TV news broadcasts. Across the industrialised world, and to a more limited extent in the developing world too, women organised themselves at work and in the public sphere, challenging the deep-seated inequalities and discriminations – some subtle, others much less so – that permeated the fabric of 'patriarchal' societies. They also experimented with forms of organisation and action that were to become staples of the anti-capitalist protests. Indeed the idea of extreme decentralisation and horizontally organised networks of like-minded groupings was something of a template for the more radically orientated direct action groupings that currently abound.

The growth of the women's movement as an unofficial form of politics was later matched by the dramatic emergence of environmental movement in the 1970s and 1980s. This was 'fuelled' in particular by the Oil Crisis of 1973, which jolted people into considering the prospect that the world's resources were not in fact unlimited as had hitherto seemed to have been assumed. United around the theme of the need to move from unsustainable growth to 'sustainable' development, the environmental movement was one of the first to generate a significant number of 'Non-Governmental Organisations' (NGOs) such as Friends of the Earth and Greenpeace (both founded in 1971). The significance of such groupings is firstly that they gave an alternative outlet for concerned or politicised individuals who had become alienated or turned off by mainstream politics. They were often highly 'professional', tightly focused, and well funded with clear, practical and largely *non-ideologically* driven purposes in mind. In a sense such groups were political 'innocents' and this was part of their attraction for those wearied by the utilitarian politicking of official parties. Nothing seemed to be hidden; there was no secret agenda and few hangers-on or cronies who had to be paid for out of hard-earned subscriptions and donations. Concerned individuals could support such causes without a sense that they were tiny cogs in some much larger power-seeking machine.

Some of these preconceptions are no doubt naïve when transferred to today's equivalents. Many NGOs would make the efforts of many minor or smaller parties look thoroughly amateurish and small time by comparison. But this is hardly the point. What *seemed* important then and still seems important now is that such groups are idealistic without being ideological, they are campaigning without being cynical; they are active not passive, which is to say that they are often the fulcrum for direct action and thus direct involvement by their members. They *do* something, rather than waiting for things to happen as often appears to be the case with political parties ('just wait until *we* get into power'). This contrast between the active and idealistic green movements and the reactive and pragmatic political establishment was at its sharpest at the Rio Earth Summit in 1992, in retrospect something akin to a rehearsal for later 'anti-capitalist' protests. Within the conference centres were rows of bemused, suited figures peddling modest proposals for reductions in emissions, saving forests, oceans and endangered species. Outside was a blur of colour, noise and vibrancy with myriad groups jostling for the attentions of the world's media, calling for radical change, wholesale transformation, and the end of an unsustainable free market capitalism. How familiar all this would become after Seattle.

The women's movement and the environmental movements were by no means the only significant new social movements to emerge in the reshaping of the political landscape after 1968. They were to be joined by an astonishing array of what are termed '*single-issue*' *groups* many of which were to become significant presences on the anti-capitalist circuit. Chief amongst these were groups campaigning on the basis of an enlargement of the sphere of rights, which over the course of the last third of the twentieth century became the dominant discourse of unofficial politics, particularly in the US. There were groups campaigning for *animal rights*, for various *human rights* particularly those focusing on gay rights, and the rights of ethnic and racial minorities to equal treatment or to 'affirmative action'. There were campaigns for the *rights of workers* in the developing world and the rights of workers in the developed world whose livelihoods were threatened by the liberalisation of the global market. There were groups campaigning for the right to immigrate, the right to health-care or drug treatments. One of the largest mobilisations in recent years was in support of those who had contracted AIDs/HIV. Vast demonstrations were held, as well as 'telethons', sit-ins, and petitions accusing the political establishment of inaction. By the end of the 1990s it seemed that the clamour of unofficial politics was almost overwhelming. And yet, still the experts and commentators talked of the boredom and 'apathy' of the 'ordinary person on the street', equating the growing reluctance of young people in particular to mandate politicians as a sign that they were somehow uninterested in politics. After Seattle there would be noticeably fewer such generalisations.

By the time of the fall of the Berlin Wall in 1989 we can already see in outline the elements shaping a new kind of oppositional politics. Its characteristics were the following:

- *It was ideologically and politically diverse.* The decline in communism, and indeed social democracy, was not matched by the emergence of a new hegemonic Idea – a new ideology that could claim to represent or embody the hopes and aspirations of those who were not accommodated within the liberal-democratic 'consensus'. There were myriad ideologies, narratives of liberation, collective demands. But there were also those motivated by *specific injustices* as opposed to the desire to create a 'just world'. This is to say there was an activism driven by non-ideological *as well as* ideological concerns. Those who protested against the abuse of animals in testing could just as well be motivated by the simple love of animals as by the desire to create a world in which the abuse of animals was, in some moral or political sense, 'impossible'.
- *It was organisationally diverse.* As the account above illustrates some groups such as the NGOs and charities were formally constituted professional or semi-professional organisations with permanent staffs and offices geared up for lobbying politicians and corporations, some of them with turnovers of many millions, large subscriber bases, glossy brochures and magazines. They could be bureaucratically organised with clear hierarchies, leaderships and professional accounting procedures. At the other end of the scale were groups constituted informally, meeting sporadically, with little of the paraphernalia of the professional lobbyists. They could be 'one event wonders', or loosely co-ordinated with some particular purpose in view. Most groups were, however, 'anti-official' politics, parties, elections. Even the NGOs kept themselves

clear of the contaminating effects of 'big politics'. Unofficial politics remained over the period unofficial, which is to say that groups
kept clear of electioneering for fear of becoming compromised by
the 'realities' of electoral politics. The major exception to this trend
were the Greens who across the globe formed themselves into
political parties as well as campaigning organisations. The pattern
of success was, however, hardly uniform. In Germany the Greens
made some breakthroughs and have participated in the highest
levels of government in recent German administrations – at the cost
of a continuing feud between deep Greens and light Greens over
the virtue of an electorally based strategy. Elsewhere the picture
was less rosy, particularly where the electoral system worked
against the emergence of minor parties, as in Britain and the US.

- *It was an active as opposed to passive style of politics.* The politics of
the new social movements was above all about participation, not
representation. One of the key themes of the politics that emerges
out of 1968 is the notion of 'being heard', whether this being heard
was in the form of consciousness-raising groups such as those
found in feminist circles, or in terms of more general notions of
interactivity and participation as found particularly in those
groups organised around the need for direct action. This was
direct action by the members of the group, not by representatives.

So at one level at least Fukuyama was right – which was in his asser-
tion that Soviet communism was in some definitive sense 'dead'. But
the assumption that oppositional politics as such was dead was
clearly flawed. Oppositional politics, a politics that took issue with
the simple contention that all was right with 'actually existing
liberal-democracy', had not gone away: far from it. As is clear, there
was a vast proliferation of 'oppositions', some ideologically driven,
others much less so; some motivated by one issue or by one set of
issues, others by a more general opposition to the *status quo*. Some
of these currents were radical and transformative in outlook; others
could be satisfied by some legal or political reform that would
remove a specific injustice. From this point of view it was easy for conservative commentators to conclude that the 'threat' to the *status quo*
had been met and defeated. There was no global movement,
no 'force' that opposed liberal-capitalism in the way that the
Soviet Union and Communist Bloc had.

It was also easy for left-wing commentators to wring their hands
and worry about the prospects for social change in the face of what

seemed like a fragmentation of political energies, and progressive causes into distinct and separate campaigns. The political thought of the 1980s and 1990s is full of such remorse, and full of attempts to hang the blame for the fragmentation on some group or another. Jürgen Habermas, the great inheritor of the quasi-Marxist tradition of Critical Theory, famously accused French 'postmodern' theorists of disarming the progressive or radical cause in their insistence on the relativity of truth and the impossibility of the reconstruction of the 'project of emancipation' around some organising principle of the sort that communism seemed to offer to an earlier generation. Others – not just 'French' theorists – revelled in the sense of fragmentation for precisely that reason, pointing out that the communist 'metanarrative' had in effect been responsible for condemning millions to the Gulag. The 'fragmentation' Habermas lamented was nothing less than the effect of the thawing of the monolithic emancipatory story, releasing voices, causes and injustices that had previously been subject to the overarching logic of the communist project. 'Plurality' and 'fragmentation' were in this sense two sides of the same coin. One person's diversity was another person's 'loss of focus' and dissipated radical energies.

If it did not quite resolve the matter, then Seattle at least gave us a glimpse of the very ideal both sets of commentators had arguably discounted, namely the emergence of a global anti-capitalist movement that was *both* diverse *and* radical, both 'fragmented' and 'united' in its common cause. The remaining question for this chapter is how do we get from this picture of plurality and fragmentation to the astonishing unity of voice heard at Seattle. What changed between 1989 and 1999?

from berlin to seattle: global anti-capitalism and the challenge to neoliberalism

Three themes are immediately pertinent here, all linked by the theme of communication. The first is that in some important sense diverse groups evidently began to identify a *common enemy*. That enemy was neoliberalism (or 'corporate power' or 'transnational capitalism' – all fingers pointing at the same target). The second point is that they exploited opportunities to communicate with each other. Here the story is one of *capacity*, of the harnessing of new technologies for the ends of common political protest. Leading on from this, thirdly, was the possibility for a kind of *global dialogue* of 'the oppressed'. How does this pan out?

neoliberalism in the sights

As regards the *common enemy*, the period immediately following 1989 saw neoliberalism break out of the narrower domestic agendas to which it had hitherto been tied. Reagan and Thatcher were both tireless *neoliberalists* in their own way, but they were largely isolated in a sea of social democratic, welfarist and quasi-collectivist systems. The world of 1989 was a very different place to that of 1999, with most governments still committed to defending the postwar 'consensus'. But with a general slow down in the world economy, and the resultant unemployment and dwindling tax revenues, the consensus exploded. This left conservative administrations to forge ahead with a fundamental restructuring, not only of their own economies, but also the trading regimes of which they were a part, all of course with the blessing of the World Bank, IMF and OECD. In 1994, for example, the US finally corralled Mexico and Canada into the North America Free Trade Area (NAFTA), allowing full penetration of corporations into hitherto untapped markets through the abolition of all impediments to trade between those within the free trade zone. In Europe the post-Maastricht negotiations focussed on the establishment of a single currency, in turn 'necessitating' policies of fiscal rectitude, balanced budgets and cuts in public expenditure. The 1990s were to be tough for labour, with millions of public sector jobs dispensed with as previously nationalised industries were led to 'the market', like so many pigs for slaughter. After a long period of retrenchment, trade unions in advanced industrial countries polarised between those who bought the rhetoric of 'TINA' and those who decided attack was the best means of defence. Some fell into line between political leaders who promised in nationalistic vein that they would safeguard jobs 'at home'. Others saw what was coming, and renewed the idealistic and internationalist credo of the labour movement. For those who had given up on the labour movement as a source of opposition, Seattle, which saw trade unionists turn out in force, surprised many both within and outside activist circles. But Seattle was perhaps also a premonition of things to come with the main bulk of trade unionists remaining on their 'official' AFL-CIO march with more militant unions such as the Steelworkers (USWA) and Longshore Workers Union (ILWU) teamed up for the historic 'turtles and teamsters' protest that grabbed the headlines.

More generally, neoliberal policies had become ubiquitous by the end of the 1990s. Even countries with a seemingly unwavering commitment to collectivist policies such as France rapidly succumbed. Indeed, it was Lionel Jospin, the ex-Trotskyite leader of the PS who ushered in a new era of 'austerity' and prudence. It suited his dour character, if not the supporters of Mitterrand's once fiercely collectivist party who turned against him in the 2002 presidential elections. The situation was, however, immeasurably more difficult around the globe where, during a brief period at the end of the 1990s, there seemed a genuine chance that the nascent global market would collapse under the weight of its own 'liquidity'. First Asia, then Russia, then South America buckled under the difficulty of maintaining political control over economic systems that, now fully open to the vagaries of speculative capital, seemed beyond the capacity of politicians to control. The sheer scale of the misery that accompanied the wild gyrations of the global economy is difficult for many of us to comprehend. What is less difficult to comprehend is the feeling of profound resentment that such conditions engendered in those who suffered as a result. If history teaches anything of relevance to our subject, it is that conditions of economic crisis can be expected to lead to political radicalisation and the search for far-reaching answers to deep-seated problems. The birth of an anti-capitalist movement was ultimately propelled by the very factors that so many western radicals had come to discount in their preference for a 'post-materialist' analysis: poverty, unemployment and powerlessness. What was perhaps notable was that economic crisis was not confined to the global 'poor'. Formerly wealthy countries felt the effects as much as their impoverished neighbours, and all compounded by an increasing sense that only a genuinely global effort could get at the cause of the collective misery.

the technological great leap-forward: the internet explosion

As regards the *capacity* of activists to organise and cross-pollinate, then the arrival of and access to advanced communications technology must be regarded as of crucial significance. Indeed, the internet has to be regarded as the most astonishing boon for activism of any technology since the arrival of the printing press or perhaps the typewriter. Why was the internet important? The internet

- gives visibility and presence to otherwise marginal groups
- facilitates the creation of activist networks
- allows greater coordination of activity
- provides alternative sources of information and news
- offers new forms of direct action ('hacktivism'; 'Net war')

Firstly and most obviously, the internet is vital in terms of giving *visibility* and *presence* to groups and causes that would otherwise remain 'hidden' from view. Before the internet, political groups relied on paper for the dissemination of their views. In the era of cheap paper and photocopiers it is not that expensive to produce leaflets, pamphlets and posters. The problem is trying to put them in places where target audiences can find them. Many booksellers and news agents are loathe to give space to such materials on commercial and ideological grounds. Numerous cases were taken out against commercial retailers for precisely these reasons in the 1970s and 1980s. Until very recently the job was done by radical and alternative bookshops or cafes usually located in major towns and cities. I used to live near the famous Compendium Bookshop in London which, as the name suggests, offered a plethora of alternative materials. Then I moved to Nottingham which doesn't have a radical book-shop. It had one, but it closed in the early 1990s. How could one get one's hands on radical material? One could subscribe, but in the fast changing world of leftist theory, what did one subscribe to? The internet changed all this. In a relatively short space of time virtually every radical or oppositional current had its presence on the web. Anyone with access could download articles, back issues of a journal, get a sense of philosophy or stance towards the great matters of the day. Moreover, the internet promotes a crude form of equality between groups. Type in 'anarchy' in a search engine and we are pre-sented with the URL addresses of tiny 'bed-sit' operations as well as large or well-organised groups such as the 'Struggle' or 'Tao' collect-ives. This can be a strength as well as a weakness in organisational terms (as we shall see); but in terms of *visibility* it transforms the potential of groups to be seen and heard.

Secondly, the internet preserved the particularity of distinct groups and causes whilst greatly facilitating the creation of *networks* of the like-minded. As well as preserving a distinct space or presence, groups could make common cause with other groups that shared their values, beliefs doctrine, priorities or purposes. This could be achieved either through a simple 'links' page which indicated which groups they felt some sense of common cause with, or through more elaborate networks, sites and mechanisms that acted as an umbrella organisation all of its own. By the end of the 1990s networks such as the Independent Media Network ('Indymedia'), People's Global Action, Global Exchange and Zmag.org were encouraging an exchange of news and views amongst activists, offering message boards, calendars of meetings and protests, contact addresses. But the significance of virtual networks and exchanges such as these went well beyond the obvious point that they permitted a flow of useful information concerning the whereabouts of protests and demonstrations. What they fostered was a form of interaction that preserved the integrity and autonomy of the constituent parts. No group was subject to the will of another. No group had to recognise one as a leading group or as the 'vanguard' of the movement. There was no need for bureaucracy, permanent staffs, officials, 'leadership', or even premises, beyond somewhere to house a server. Here was a form of interaction that denied the need for the very institutional and logistical framework that had for a century defined the terms and conditions of political activism. It enacted a form of electronic anarchy, a literal free-for-all in which anyone with access to the necessary equipment could make their presence 'felt'. The internet encouraged a version of the commons to come to life, a 'space/place' that was largely ungoverned and ungovernable either by corporate interests or by would-be revolutionary leaders and parties. Governments and corporations could watch and spy on internet activists, but they couldn't control or eliminate them.

Thirdly, the internet permitted the *coordination of activity* along the above lines. This is to say that activists now had a means of marshalling activism along the same anarchistic lines that underpinned the growth of the internet itself. One group could alert many other groups to the existence of a movement of nuclear waste, to the shutting of a factory, to the destruction of an ecologically sensitive site, to the arrival of US military personnel. It could suggest a time, place and appropriate form of direct action. It could smooth the activist task and give a sense of solidarity to those who might otherwise wonder what awaited. It made activism logistically easier, if not less risky. Just looking at the preparations for the G8 summit at Evian in May 2003, the 'hosts' (www.nadir.org) posted various suggestions for accommodation (including squats), maps of the town and area, a suggested timetable for various forms of protests and demonstrations, coordination centres, email addresses for organisers and also for those against whom the protests were taking place, suggestions for parties and social activities. None of this is in any way 'binding' in the sense that it prevents any given group conducting its own form of protest. Rather it represents the effort to produce forms of collective action that are effective but without, at the same time, reducing the individuality or autonomy of the constituent elements. What the internet fostered was thus the *crystallisation* of activism whilst preserving the particularity of the actors themselves. It is difficult to think of such a precedent in the long history of political activism.

Fourthly, the internet offers an alternative source of news and information. In an era where media ownership has progressively narrowed to a handful of mega-conglomerates, the internet provides a vital alternative perspective on global events. As print media becomes ever more dumbed-down in the hunt for the lowest common denominator, internet-based news gathering, the sharing of informal news and reporting becomes ever-more important, not just to activists, but to anyone wanting an alternative 'take' on global events and developments. But it is not just the content that is important, it is also the speed with which events can be narrated and relayed to networks of activists and those more generally concerned about global politics. Needless to say the level of information and analysis is uneven to say the least; but the ability of otherwise voiceless groups and minorities to interact with a global audience has been one of the keys to the development of anti-capitalism as a global phenomenon. It has increased the awareness of groups of each other and permitted the exchange of stories, strategies, tactics in mutual solidarity.

Finally, one of the most commented upon aspects of the growth of the internet has been the growth of *internet-based direct action* as a supplement to more conventional forms of protesting. In a twist on the 'subvertising' theme discussed above, the websites of corporations and government agencies have been attacked, with home pages altered in judicious ways to subvert the official 'welcome'. Even the CIA's website has suffered from the attentions of the hacktivists despite their preoccupation with security in the era of 'Netwar'. There have been episodes of 'cyber-squatting' in which hackers have occupied the servers of ill-fated organisations, refusing to 'move' until they have been heard. There have been myriad email protests directed at corporate targets. We can also mention the practice of 'pinging', where servers are attacked by message auto-replies that swamp the home server to the point where they are disabled. Whilst the effect of such actions is often uncertain, what they illustrate is, nevertheless, the increasing multiplicity of ways in which people can be heard, can act, can 'do' something even if the effect of the 'doing' is perhaps more difficult to measure than more traditional forms of activism.

towards a global (anti-capitalist) village

Finally, we need to link all of these points to the emergence of a genuinely *global dialogue* of those concerned about the state of the world. We have already mentioned the Rio Summit of 1992 which provided a template for future struggles, but if we are thinking in terms of the movement when a global resistance to anti-capitalism was born then arguably it would be the moment in 1994 when the Zapatistas dramatically emerged out of the forests of south-eastern Mexico to declare the Chiapas region an autonomous zone. There were two ways in which their arrival seemed so significant. The first was the sense in which their actions were inspired as much by developments in the global economy as in the injustices and indignities to which the indigenous people of the region had been subjected. Their arrival immediately followed the signing of the NAFTA agreement which consigned Mexico to the mercies of the corporations. Whilst the agreement was not the *cause* of the Zapatista actions it nonetheless provided a more than merely symbolic backdrop for their actions. As quickly became apparent, the Zapatista agenda was much broader than that of a 'rebel' force with few concerns beyond securing greater justice for some hitherto neglected constituency, the indigenous peasants of the Chiapas. Rather they saw the significance of their actions in wider terms, seeing their struggle as part of the global struggle against neoliberalism. Here again, the significance of the internet which permitted the Zapatistas to communicate with other activists via the Indymedia exchange, with up-dates on their activities, campaigns and photos, is apparent.

Others have followed in their wake. Sem Terra, the movement of the landless in Brazil which seeks to reappropriate unused lands for cooperative farming, has similarly become a globally recognised organisation through its high visibility and use of advanced information technology to inform activists about its campaigns, to call for donations, and coordinate 'actions' with others. In this sense it is now difficult to regard the struggles of even peasant-based movements like Sem Terra as merely 'local'. They interact with others; they attend the major events and protests of the travelling anti-capitalist circus; and they have representatives and delegates at the various social forums held around the world. The local has become the global, just as the global, in terms of corporate rule, commercial-isation and the disappearance of the 'commons' has become local.

In the wake of the economic crisis of 1997 activism of all kinds was on the rise across the developing as well as developed world. In East Asia, in Africa, Latin America and the Middle East militancy was on the upsurge, much of it bolstered by the sense of solidarity that it was now possible for others to express. Strange alliances, curious affiliations and lines of sympathy opened up, mostly as a result of the fact that people were able to hear about and anticipate struggles before they were even 'news events'. The opening up of a global internet-based dialogue persuaded many that they were not 'alone', that there others who had the same problems as them, and that those problems stemmed from the same source: the stranglehold on lives and livelihoods exercised by the global elites. Shared prognosis led to ideas of a shared resistance and thus to the idea of a global anti-capitalist movement centred on the oppressed, poor and marginal of the world.

conclusion

So oppositional politics did not go away. It went underground. But what is interesting is the way in which 'the underground' itself changed in radical ways in a short space of time. 'Underground' no longer meant 'hidden from view', 'without the means of communi-cation' or just 'isolated'. Underground now implied a vast network of interactivity, 'hidden' from the daily newshounds, but nonetheless resurgent and in some cases as we have seen insurgent. Seattle was the moment when in a sense the rest of the world was made aware of the sheer scope and extensiveness of the network. But it is difficult not to conclude that it was the moment when the activist commu-nity *itself* latched on to the idea that this network-based activism could be something more than a gesture of solidarity for the other-wise disparate struggles with which each of these groups had been engaged. There was a quite palpable change in the consciousness not only of those who bore the brunt of activism – mainly the corporations and the global elites – but also of those who were engaged in the actions themselves. Something snowballed and it was not just the sense or scope of the protests themselves. After Seattle activists and commentators began to take seriously the idea that there was indeed an anti-capitalist movement. Yet they knew what they were against: neoliberalism. What was more difficult to get a handle on was what the movement was *for*. Was the movement really to be a movement, or a vast structure of connected and interconnected groups and causes? Was it to have a wider agenda or programme which it could offer as an alternative to contemporary capitalism? Curious to say, with Seattle the 'easy' part was over. 'Anti-capitalism' had arrived. But where was it going?

resources

read on

Harry Cleaver, 'Computer-linked Social Movements and the Global Threat to Capitalism', www.eco.utexas.edu/homepages/faculty/Cleaver/polnet.html

Alexander Cockburn and Jeffrey St Clair, *Five Days that Shook the World: The Battle for Seattle and Beyond* (London and New York: Verso, 2000).

Guy Debord, *The Society of the Spectacle* (London: Rebel Press, 1971 [1967]). Full text available online at: www.library.nothingness.org/articles/SI/en/pub_contents/4

Jo Freeman, 'On the Origins of Social Movements', www.jofreeman.com/socialmovements/origins.htm

Francis Fukuyama, 'The End of History?', *The National Interest*, 16 (Summer 1989), pp. 3–18 – followed by *The End of History and the Last Man* (London and New York: Penguin, 1992).

Jürgen Habermas, 'Modernity versus Postmodernity', *New German Critique*, no. 22 (1981), pp. 3–14.

Axel Hadenius (ed.), *Democracy's Victory and Crisis* (Cambridge: Cambridge University Press, 1997).

Eric Hobsbawm, *The New Century* (London: Abacus, 2000).

Jean-François Lyotard, *The Postmodern Condition* (Minneapolis: University of Minnesota Press, 1984).

Herbert Marcuse, *One-Dimensional Man* (Boston: Beacon Press, 1966).

Anthony Oberschall, *Social Movements: Ideologies, Interest, and Identities* (London: Transaction Publishers, 1993).

Sadie Plant, *The Most Radical Gesture: The Situationist International in a Postmodern Age* (London: Routledge, 1992).

Angelo Quattrochi and Tom Nairn, *The Beginning of the End: France, May 1968* (London and New York: Verso, 1998).

Theodore Roszak, *The Making of a Counter-Culture: Reflections on the Technocratic Society and its Youthful Opposition* (Berkeley: University of California Press, 1993).

Donald Sassoon, *One Hundred Years of Socialism* (London: Fontana, 1996).

Raoul Vaneigem, *The Revolution of Everyday Life* (London: Rebel Press, 1994 [1967]). Full text available online at: www.library.nothingness.org/articles/SI/en/pub_contents/5

Immanuel Wallerstein, 'New Revolts Against the System', *New Left Review*, 18 (Nov.–Dec. 2002) available online at: www.newleftreview.net/NLR 25202. shtml

link to

www.nothingness.org (situationist texts)
www.newleftreview.net
www.subvertise.org
www.adbusters.org
www.greenpeace.org
www.foe.org (friends of the earth, USA)
www.foe.co.uk
www.indymedia.org
www.hacktivismo.org
www.cultdeadcow.com (hacktivist site and portal)
www.globalexchange.org
www.bak.spc.org/j18/site/ (activist grouping J18's exchange site)
www.nadir.org (People's Global Action)
www.jofreeman.com (articles on Women's lib; radical social movements)
www.mstbrazil.org (Sem Terra)

a 'movement of movements'

i: 'reformism', or 'globalisation with a human face'

At the end of the last chapter we noted that in the wake of the protests against the meeting of the WTO in Seattle, it became customary to speak in terms of the existence of an 'anti-capitalist' – or sometimes 'anti-globalisation' – movement. Yet there are many difficulties in getting to grips with the nature of this movement, one that seemed to many to appear from nowhere. One of the immediate problems is how to delineate 'anti-capitalism' itself, which we shall now do in Part I of our analysis of the 'movement of movements'. Do we start thinking in terms of all those who are or have been present at various protests and carnivals where anti-capitalists meet? In other words, do we try to define anti-capitalism primarily by reference to distinct *events*, examining in sociological style the various 'presences' at Seattle, Genoa, Quebec? Or, do we think more in terms of the *ideas* of those who describe themselves as 'anti-capitalist' or who in some other way associate themselves with the anti-capitalist struggles, for example by participating at the World Social Forums, by demonstrating in support of the landless peasants of Brazil or the sweatshop workers of Southeast Asia?

As is clear, the two overlap to a certain extent in the sense that many of those who turn up to protests, who consider themselves activists, are at the same time those whose animosity to capitalism is driven by certain ideas about how the world should look. But not everyone who turns up to anti-capitalist protests is 'anti-capitalist' in this sense, and quite a lot are not. One should never discount those who have bunked off school for a day, *agents provocateurs*, free loaders,

GENOA – WHAT HAPPENED?

The meeting of the G8 In Genoa scheduled for July 2001 provided the pretext for a massive series of demonstrations and a concomitant massive increase in policing. Indeed Genoa was in many respects the high tide of a certain conception of 'protest activism' involving demos of ever-increasing size and dynamism in an effort to press home popular discontent with the nature and form of global capitalism. It also represented, quite literally, the death of a certain innocence about the nature and form of protests, for the police reacted to the demonstrators with a savagery yet to be matched at other protests in the industrialised world. Carlo Guiliani, a young Italian protester, was killed when he attempted to attack a Police van. A young carabinieri shot him directly in the head before the vehicle ran over Guiliani whose dying body lay on the street. Later on riot police raided the Indymedia Centre at Diaz School, laying waste to everyone and everything they found within. 'Weapons' were paraded the next day, providing a justification for actions that finally confirmed the 'different' character of Genoa. More generally, Genoa will be remembered not just for the brutality of the police, but also for the recriminations that broke out between the various groupings and factions present. In particular the activities of the Black Bloc, a loose coalition of militant activists attached to the use of 'symbolic' violence, prompted a great deal of soul-searching amongst activists. Genoa was very palpably a turning point for the movement, which now somehow had to decide how best to promote anti-capitalist ideas without allowing the authorities to turn 'carnivals' into carnage.

the curious, sensation-seekers, indeed sociologists and academics studying the nature of contemporary 'protest'. Some change their minds because of what they hear at the protests. Some in other words may arrive at a protest as a representative of a trade union, or as a single issue activist, and become committed to a more radical position because they have become convinced that the best way of advancing trade union causes or to confront specific injustices is to oppose corporate or neoliberal capitalism. Protests, marches and demonstrations have never in this sense been mere passive aggregates of individuals, but are also moments when people learn about the grievances and beliefs of others. Indeed if the anti-capitalist phenomenon can be credited with one thing it is this very evidently *educative* function that meetings and protests have performed. A lot of people have learned an awful lot about the condition of other people, and in turn have learned to see themselves and their apparently discrete causes as merely part of a more general problematic. On the other hand, what is also evident is that many people who consider themselves anti-capitalist in some general way do not take part in the various anti-capitalist protests. This includes many who are too poor to travel, those who are compelled to work on a particular day in question, those who for some reason cannot face crowds or potentially violent gatherings, those in prison, those with child-care responsibilities or some other commitment that keeps them away. 'Anti-capitalism' must in this sense be more than the spectacle. It must be about ideas. Without ideas there can be no 'event'. More seriously, without ideas there can be no debate on the 'after' of capitalism. Ultimately if we want to understand anti-capitalism we need to understand what it is that anti-capitalism is as a set of *ideas*.

Even if we accept that what we should be looking at are anti-capitalist ideas, further problems follow, for what is even more evident is the degree to which 'anti-capitalism' is a mere umbrella term for myriad causes, ideologies, movements, parties and world views. It is for this reason that many who try to describe the nature of anti-capitalism now tend to describe it as a 'movement of movements'. Anti-capitalism lacks many of the characteristics that defined movements of the past. In particular it lacks a unifying ideology or programme. There are no 'holy books', no doctrine or philosophy to which one can refer to get a sense of a core orientation. Nor is there a leader, considered either in charismatic, doctrinal or in organisational terms. There are certainly important, even 'iconic', figures. We could mention here Subcomandante Marcos of the Zapatistas, who seems to be approaching Che Guevara in terms of his symbolic status for the movement of movements. One can even buy 'Marcos' T-shirts at tourist 'hot-spots' around the world depicting his now famous hooded profile, complete with pipe and pensive expression. There are others such as Naomi Klein, Walden Bello, Susan George, Noam Chomsky, Toni Negri, José Bové and Mumia Abu-Jamal who have a high profile amongst activists. But they do not lead in the sense that Lenin led the Bolsheviks in 1917 or Mussolini the Fascists in the March on Rome. This is a remarkably, perhaps thankfully, *leader-less* movement, once again underlining the degree to which as we noted in the last chapter groups and parties lead their own separate and equal existence.

It follows that if we wish to understand anti-capitalism as a set of ideas then we have to accept the central fact about it, namely that 'it', the movement of movements, is composed of *disaggregated, plural and competing conceptions* of how capitalism is to be combated and changed. Indeed anti-capitalism is defined as much by the *differences* between the various elements composing the 'whole' as by the *similarities.* To say it is a movement of movements is to say that it is composed of distinct groupings or molecules each with its own agenda, passions and constituency. Whether the anti-capitalist movement can be *effective* as a 'molecular' as opposed to 'molar' structure is a question to which we will need to return. All we can note here is that up to the present theorists of resistance have assumed that there is a necessary correlation between the 'unity' of political purpose of a movement and its effectivity. The assumption is that without a certain agreement on ends and means, there is no movement as such, 'only' a 'movement of movements', an umbrella beneath which otherwise irreconcilable causes and groups may temporarily shelter before moving on. It follows from the above that in order to get a sense of the prospects of anti-capitalism we need to get a sense of the discrete groups that compose the 'it' in question, what it is they offer in terms of an analysis of the present state of the world and in terms of a prescription for the future state of the world. Who are the anti-capitalists?

analysing anti-capitalist ideas: beginnings

In attempting to think about the ideological commitments of a heterogeneous movement of this kind there is considerable temptation to reach for a rather tired tool of political analysis, the 'left-right spectrum'. This is to say that we think in terms of a one dimensional plane with 'radical' at one end and 'reformers' at the other. We then plot the various tendencies of the movement on the plane and in such fashion depict the differences in ideology and strategy along it. There is a certain sense in which this has a validity here, but only a certain sense. Looking at the anti-capitalist movement in disaggregated terms we do indeed see very radical groups, less radical groups and not very radical groups, all in the same political 'space'. So much will be obvious to anyone who has been privy to the efforts of anti-capitalists to agree on a programme for change, particularly those who keep up with the politics of the World Social Forum, the 'umbrella' group set up in 2001, one of whose purposes is to generate an agreed platform with which to advance 'the cause'. The left/right spectrum is, however, too simplistic for our purposes. What it leaves out is just as important as what is left in, which is the fact that many groupings within the anti-capitalist movement are evidently either *non-ideological* or *post-ideological*. This is to say that there are groupings that are quite explicitly opposed to the idea that what the movement needs is an alternative vision of how the world should look. For them, opposition to capitalism, or neoliberalism, stems from the fact that capitalism imposes a vision of the world thereby making impossible other forms of life, other ways of living, other visions, other kinds of social interaction, other ways of organising communities. To be *non* or *post*-ideological is in this sense to hold over the task of sketching out 'the future' or the best world or the most desirable form of life to some later moment – if at all. It is, as it were, to leave the canvas blank, or rather to rescue the canvas from those who are busy filling it up with gaudy colours of global consumerism.

This is by contrast to *ideologically-driven* groupings that histor-ically have counter-posed the present to some ideal or, in any case, a much better alternative. The great tendency of post-Enlightenment political thought has been of this nature. Starting from some account of human nature, some notion of human needs or wants, some conception of social progress of historical development, thinkers have generated a critique of the given states of affairs based on a superior idea of how the world could look. Thinking back to the first chapter we can see such an operation at work very clearly in the thought of Hayek and Friedman. Both had a strong sense of where the world had gone wrong and what measures were needed to make it better. People need markets to express themselves and to help social reproduction. Thus the more 'market' we have the better. It is for this reason that we talk about neoliberal*ism*. An 'ism' is a complete package. It contains an *analysis* of the present combined with a *prescription* for future happiness, well-being, progress.

As is clear, 'anti-capitalism' is not like 'neoliberalism' in this sense. There isn't one anti-capitalist ideology, but many anti-capitalisms. Not only that there are not only various ideological currents, but there are also forms of activism and different types of grouping that consciously eschew 'ideology' altogether. What is evident is that the anti-capitalist movement is composed *both* of radicals and reformists, and *also* composed of groups with strong ideological affiliations and identities and others that quite self-consciously lack such attachments. This suggests the need to dispense with a simple or horizontal left/right spectrum and instead to think in terms of, at the very least, a two dimensional typology with a further vertical plane. Our analysis would maintain a horizontal plane with the most radical groups at one end leading to the most reformist at the other; but we would intersect that plane with a vertical axis. On the vertical we could place ideological or 'affirmative' groups closer to the top and non/post-ideological groups near the bottom.

If all this sounds a little clinical and cut-and-dried, it is. The picture is actually much more complex, as will become apparent. Indeed one of the factors that cannot be represented diagrammatically is the presence of *single-issue groups, NGOs, and religious lobbyists,* many of which are not in fact anti-capitalist *at all.* What also escapes representation is that many umbrella groupings are themselves composed of more or less homogenous groupings. ATTAC, one of the highest profile groupings at global level, quickly moved from a relatively homogenous grouping to one that embraces all manner of currents and tendencies, some radical, some much less

A two-dimensional typology of anti-capitalist positions

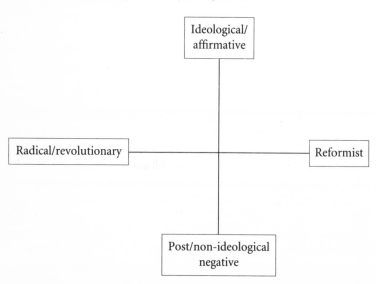

so. A cross-sectional analysis, however, at least gives us a *relatively* intelligible picture of the different ideological dimensions at work in the movement. It also gives us a sense of one or two important fault lines running across the movement, namely that between radicals and reformers, *and* that between groups whose opposition to capitalism stems from a prior ideological vantage point and those whose opposition stems from the desire to counter or negate an ideology, namely neoliberalism.

Over the next two chapters I will try to give a sense of how these affiliations operate in practice. In the next chapter we look at the 'radical' wing of anti-capitalism. We begin, however, by looking at the reformist wing. I should make clear at this point that my interest in using the terms 'reformist' and 'radical' is merely as loose descriptors for different kinds of commitments. It is not my intention to imply that one position is implicitly or explicitly more valid than the other, though of course they *do* have this connotation in the infra-struggles of the anti-capitalist movement itself. For Marxists, 'reformists' are people who invariably 'sell out' to capitalism. Yet 'reformist' positions may well seem quite radical to those who have given little thought to the nature of global capitalism, though the implementation of reformist policies will involve less radical measures than the wholesale transformation of global structures demanded by many on the radical wing. This is only to be expected. Nonetheless what is meant by 'radical' here is a commitment to *a substantial or complete transformation of global capitalism*. Radicals are those who *actually* want to rid the world of capitalism, which, as will be recalled from chapter one, involves getting rid of the private ownership of the means of production, whether presided over by corporations or not. It stands for the abolition of production for profit and of the institution of wage labour. This, as will be apparent, is a tall order, some would say an impossibly utopian one, involving a complete or fundamental break with the present. Whether it would require a 'revolution' in the formal sense of an overthrowing of the current global order is a very heated topic and one to which (again) we shall return in due course. Here, however, we discuss the ideas of those whose view of 'anti-capitalism' falls short of the fundamental transformation called for by radical groups. They typically oppose *corporate* capitalism, but not capitalism as such. Very generally, they are looking to break the spell of a particular kind of globalisation, namely the neoliberal variety. They are not ideologically or pragmatically committed to a 'post-capitalist' vision of global economic organisation, but rather to an amelioration of current conditions for the benefit of those who have been excluded or poorly served by economic globalisation. As will be apparent, this leaves a lot of possibilities open, so we need, firstly, to find some labels on which we can hang the myriad forms of reformist position. How to proceed?

'strong' and 'weak' (liberal) reformisms

It is probably true to say that most people who have been present at anti-capitalist protests and marches are not in fact 'anti-capitalist' on a strict reading of the term – particularly the protests held in North America. These are people of whom we might say that they are anti-globalisation, or anti-corporations, or they might not be anti- anything very large and 'abstract' such as 'capitalism' as such. However, it is true to say that anti-capitalist demonstrations are full of people who are opposed to what we have been calling *specific injustices*, such as a lack of rights for workers, or animals or indigenous peoples. They are also full of representatives of NGOs whose job it is to remedy specific injustices or to draw attention to discrete areas of policy making that require the attention of global elites, such as the condition of the environment, the supply of clean water or the need to abolish debt. To demonstrate against a specific injustice is to demonstrate against a *symptom* of global capitalism, something that is produced by global capitalism. Most of the time the call for the relief of such symptoms does not involve a threat or challenge to the global capitalist order itself, but rather a *limitation* on the capacity of capitalists to act in particular ways. Yet even the desire to limit capitalism is in some sense 'anti-capitalist' as capitalism is now constituted, that is as 'neoliberal' capitalism. This is because (as we discussed in chapter one) the thrust of neoliberalism is towards a *minimisation* of political constraints on the market. Neoliberals are interested in taking away limitations to the actions of capitalists. Anything that seeks either to reimpose limitations or to call for new ones is regarded as a threat to the 'self-regulating market order' that underpins the 'Washington consensus'. Thus, even modest forms of interventionism have been rendered 'anti-capitalist' even where activists and lobbyists are reluctant to see themselves in such terms. The view that the task of the anti-capitalist or anti-globalisation movement is primarily to constrain or limit the actions of capitalists can, however, be more or less ideologically based. When it is ideological it resembles what might be termed '*liberal internationalism*'. When it is less ideologically driven it might be termed '*liberal interventionism*'. Let's start with the latter which would on our typology represent the bottom right hand corner and then work our way up to more ideologically derived forms.

liberal interventionism and the search for a 'compassionate globalisation'

Thinking in terms of what a non or liberal interventionism offers, it is clear that such a position equates to the view that, whilst the global order is far from perfect, the means of remedying many of the more significant injustices of the world are already in place or are in the process of being brought into being. Reformers, which include the UN itself (particularly the UN Development Programme), many NGOs and elements of the global elite such as George Soros, Ted Turner and Bill Gates, start from the successful establishment of the post-1945 settlement, pointing to the manner in which institutions of global social and political governance have established an international order to which the vast majority of the world's nations have signed up. Others, including Bill Clinton and Tony Blair, focus on the shared 'values' they see as part of the postwar order, with its stress on the enlargement of the sphere of human rights and the necessity for responsible governance. For interventionists the problem is that such calls have all too often fallen on deaf ears when it comes to global corporations. This is to say that, whilst the discourse of human rights and common thresholds of decency as regards standards of living across the world have largely been accepted by policymakers and forums such as the UN, corporations have been slow to respond in kind. Indeed, the record up to the present has been poor with environmental degradation, human rights abuses, sweatshop labour and child workforces all too often the price to be paid for keeping profit margins high. Thus the interventionist exhorts corporations to develop mission statements and 'charters' professing their attachment to certain thresholds of 'decency' and respect for workers and environment. Clinton's emotive calls for a 'reformed' globalisation and Blair's similar call for 'compassionate' globalisation thus focused on the need for better links between labour and capital, for minimum rights for workers and limited debt relief. Clinton and Blair are not, of course, 'anti-globalisation'; but what they are calling for is in its own way similar to what many of those who do identify with such a position call for: a shift in the 'culture' of global capitalism from a rapacious, anarchic free-for-all to an 'orderly' and 'decent' process that benefits the poor and needy rather than seeing them as so much fodder for profit maximisation.

As we noted in chapter one, there is indeed a significant difference between the post-war order and earlier colonial and then imperial ages. Most nations can't do *exactly* what they want; similarly most companies can't do *exactly* what they want. To the interventionist, such observations are significant: nations and corporations have to obey – or be seen to obey – the legal and political framework which was set up after 1945 to regulate and limit the behaviour of national and supra-national actors. Not to do so would incur the prospect of being *shamed* into compliance by the insistence of international actors and global civil society that the culture as well as the letter of the rule of law be 'respected'. Protesting is a process of shaming according to this view. It is also a process of *lobbying* to have these powers extended and augmented by firmer controls, more laws where none exist, and to strengthen the capacity of the international order to regulate itself in accordance with them. Sometimes specific injustices are the result of the inadequacy of *existing legislation* and controls, and sometimes they are the result of inadequate or ineffective *implementation*. Liberal interventionism is in essence the view that existing legislation has to be strengthened along with the machinery for its implementation. Thus liberal interventionist demands are typically issued in the form of 'rights'. Workers need more rights – but so do turtles and indigenous peoples. This in turn presupposes a 'neutral' sovereign power that is able to enforce existing rights and propose new ones. Hence the central role that supra-national institutions play in liberal discourse generally. Nation states and corporations cannot be trusted because they have 'interests' they are zealous to protect. Supra-national bodies like the UN, on the other hand, were set up to represent everyone's 'interests' and thus can be charged with carrying out this neutral function – so it is hoped.

A much debated example that illustrates the strengths and weaknesses of the approach is the issue of pollution and more specifically of global warming which have been at the forefront of environmentally based activism for some decades. The Rio Summit of 1992 saw protesters attempting to draw the attention of the world's media and elites to the matter, resulting in an agreement to attempt to diminish greenhouse gases. Many of the world's powers agreed to meet at the Kyoto summit in December 1997 to work out a format by which harmful emissions could be reduced, thereby helping to contain global warming. The willingness of the world's rulers to meet demonstrates the reformers point, i.e. that effective action to off-set the worst effects of rampant global development could be success-fully lobbied for. On the other hand, the United States subsequently withdrew from the Kyoto accord, arguing that the measures recom-mended were not based on scientific 'fact'. It also argued that the proposals would harm industry and in turn cause unemployment and a global slow down, which would in turn be bad for the economies of the developing world. The failure of Kyoto thus high-lights both the strength and weakness of liberal interventionism. That the global elite sat down at all to debate how to confront a pressing environmental problem shows that with sufficient pressure they can be made to listen, and indeed 'act' in order to bring about changes to the legal and political framework. The fact that the US was able to hamper the implementation of the accords shows that, at present, US elites feel themselves sufficiently immune to such pres-sures to prefer defending their own interests and the interests of 'business' over the interests of the rest of the world. The answer according to liberal interventionists is not, however, to give up the strategy of bringing pressure to bear on the US administration or indeed on the corporations that help shape US foreign policy. It is rather to intensify pressure on this and the myriad other issues of concern to those with specific injustices to be remedied – whether that be the condition of sweatshops, the lack of fresh water supplies or the creation of greenhouse gases. Liberal interventionism there-fore requires us to accept that:

- the particular and general interests of capital can be challenged by concerted pressure exercised 'from below', namely through protests, demonstrations, petitions and lobbying. Corporations can be made to feel 'guilty' at betraying core or common values appearing in their mission statements and advertising. Capitalism can be made more 'caring' and more responsible both to con-sumer and producer needs.
- the primary function of international institutions is to regulate international affairs in accordance with what is just and reasonable as opposed to what is in the interests of corporations or big business. The UN is not an 'arm' of capital, but a genuinely

independent court of appeal and lobbying organisation which,
with some reforms, could be an effective weapon in the struggle
against the abuse of the world's poor and weak.

- the position of the US as global 'hegemon' and as carrier of an
ultimate 'veto' against 'progressive' measures is a potentially
positive as well as negative factor in world affairs, offering the
prospect that the US *could* underpin measures designed to benefit
the whole – but only when led by enlightened *multilateralists* or
left Democrats (like Clinton) – not narrow *unilateralists* or
neoliberals such as Reagan and Bush Jnr.
- US politics is itself amenable to pressure from below to alter
foreign as well as domestic policy in accordance with liberal
principles as opposed to the interests of capital. The job of
activists is continually to point to the discrepancy between what
the US *says* it stands for and what it *does* or allows to take place
in its 'name'.

In their defence liberal interventionists can point to some significant
successes. The extensive sweatshop campaigns organised across US
campuses have signally embarrassed corporations such as Nike and
Gap, and compelled them to take seriously the threat of boycotts
and consumer 'strikes'. As Klein documents in *No Logo*, such brands
trade on their street credibility and sensitivity to the needs and aspirations of youth. Thus when 'youth' is mobilised against them (as
they have done to an increasing degree in the US and elsewhere),
they have to sit up and take notice. Campaigns such as these play
capitalism's self-image against itself. They point to the contradictions inherent in the 'promise' of the brand, thereby provoking –
at least potentially – a consumer backlash and thus a threat to their
profit margin. What they don't do is (according to critics) challenge
the right of capitalism to hire labour or make huge profits out of the
efforts of its reserve army labouring away in the tax-free, unregu-
lated havens of the global South. Direct action of this kind also
serves to highlight discrepancies between the values and ideals of the
American political imaginary ('equality'; the 'Dream'; 'freedom')
against the reality of global misery and exploitation. As contemporary US history shows, progressive advances can and are made on the
basis of exploiting this gap between the 'promise' and 'reality' of US
policy. Change might not occur as fast as radicals would like, and it
might not go as far as critics demand. Nonetheless, without direct
action of this kind the position of ethnic and racial minorities, of

women, of the poor, would in all probability be immeasurably worse than it is now – and this is to say nothing about actions against specific injustices such as the Vietnam War which contributed to the decision to pull out.

we love the UN: 'liberal internationalism' and the future of global governance

Although many activists in the US would fall into the non-ideologically driven interventionist camp, there is a strong tradition both in the US and elsewhere, particularly Europe, of a more ideologically orientated form of reformism, the strains of which can occasionally be heard in the pronouncements, not just of activists, but also NGOs, elites, academics and media figures. This would be what we are calling liberal or 'cosmopolitan' internationalism. The work of the philosopher Immanuel Kant who lived at the end of the eighteenth century remains the clearest statement of such a position, so it is worth briefly outlining his own much-imitated account of 'globalisation'.

Kant considered himself a kind of realist in the sense that he regarded peoples and nations as characterised by what he termed 'unsocial sociability'. This is to say that he thought the primary dynamic of social life to be underpinned by our desire to realise our own 'ends', that is to secure our own wants and needs. These ends often clashed or contradicted the ends of others, necessitating rules and laws and thus institutions guaranteeing a certain freedom of movement and action. Obeying these laws was regarded by Kant as the necessary price for social peace and our continuing capacity to act as 'autonomous' or free individuals. Kant saw the problem of global peace as essentially analogous to the problem of social peace. Different nations and cultures co-exist, each as a limit to, as well as a means for, the realisation of the other's ends. This necessitates a system of international institutions that allow each nation or state to realise its own ends without having to submit to the threats or blandishments of the others. Such a conception was, we can add, very much at the forefront of the thinking of the founders of the UN. Relations between states had to be guided by laws which each would seek to live by to the benefit of the whole. It is thus implicit to a Kantian approach that global institutions be strong enough to countermand the instructions and edicts of national institutions. It is also implicit that the relationship between global political institutions and economic institutions should weigh in favour of the former rather than the latter, and indeed that the latter should *themselves* come to be 'political' as opposed to narrowly economic in terms of character and function.

Kant's prognosis directly and indirectly underpins the position of those whose greatest concern is with the 'democratic deficit' we remarked on in chapter one. As we noted there, global governance is currently characterised firstly by the predominance of economic considerations over political issues, which in turn reflects the neo-liberal belief in the priority of the market over the public sphere. To put the same matter differently, global politics is not really 'political' at all in the sense that issues of global justice, of welfare and redistribution, are signally absent from the agendas of global institutions, and particularly those whose function has been expressed in narrowly 'economic' terms, such as the IMF and World Bank. It is also characterised by the non-democratic nature of global institutions generally, making them amenable to the wishes of the most powerful capitalist states as well as to transnational capital. As becomes evident, it is legitimate to regard such a position as 'anti-capitalist' in the sense that in calling for the *re-politicisation* of the realm of the economy, liberal internationalism calls for economic matters to become subject to political decision-making, which in turn directly contradicts the thrust of neoliberal orthodoxy. Assuming those political institutions were to become democratic then this would open the way to a challenge to the rights of capitalists to organise their affairs with no care except for profit maximisation and accumulation. All these specific injustices, for example would then have an outlet for their expression within the institutions themselves, allowing a full and continuous debate on the nature and course of global economic matters.

On the other hand, what is rarely suggested by those propounding such an approach is that capitalism itself should be overthrown or transformed. What is suggested rather is that neoliberal capitalism could be contested both regionally and at global level by other models of capitalist development, in particular those permitting the setting of politically driven goals and objectives. In practice therefore, it is impossible to say whether institutional reform would of itself bring about a significant change to the structure of the global economy. This would be to prejudge the outcome of democratic deliberation itself. Indeed, if global institutional reform were merely to follow the line of *national* institutional reform – of the sort seen across nation states at the end of the eighteenth century – then there would be little reason to think that the pattern of private ownership over production would necessarily alter in very significant ways. The 'democratic revolution' did not challenge the rights of property owners in America or France, but rather helped shape institutions and procedures that were very much in their interests. This illustrates why such an approach has to be considered as *mildly* reformist. Internationalist approaches call for institutional reform and change, and not for change and reform in the character of capitalist production itself. But we still need to get clear about what is on offer. What is institutional reform? How might this work?

Many reformists point to the non-democratic and unrepresenta-tive nature of global institutions. Although the vast majority of states are represented on these bodies, their 'voices' are heavily differenti-ated in favour of the major states of the North. Thus the UK, the US, France, China and Russia are all permanent members of the UN Security Council, whereas all other countries merely rotate, thereby ensuring that the interests of the major economic powers are para-mount as regards issues of global security. At the IMF and the World Bank the distribution of votes, and thus of influence and power, follows the quota of funds that a given country makes available to it. Again, the result is that the voices of the US, the UK, France and other major states is dominant, which in turn means that corporate interests and the interests of the North come before those of the developing world. The G8, in which the eight wealthiest countries in the world come together to discuss matters of shared concern, is by definition a 'rich man's club' excluding the voices of poorer coun-tries. Despite being based on the more egalitarian principle of 'one nation, one vote', the WTO's *rationale* is quite explicitly to promote 'free trade' and 'open markets', thereby ruling out rival conceptions of global development. Most of its decisions are in any case the result of behind-the-scenes bargaining in the fabled 'green room' between countries of the wealthy North keen to maintain their privileged position in world trade. The World Economic Forum (WEF) is an informally constituted private association of wealthy corporations meeting annually at Davos in Switzerland to discuss how best to protect their own interests. It does not even pretend to 'represent' the interests of the poor and needy, as opposed to its wealthy clientele that pays to attend. The result is that at global level there is an implicit and sometimes explicit consensus in favour of measures that favour the large corporations who have a strong voice in determining the domestic agendas of political parties in the developed world. Reform of the institutions thus focuses on two issues: the first is the *composition* of international bodies, and the second on their *role*.

In terms of *composition*, the argument advanced by institutional reformers is that, if the developing world was given more of a say in the running of global institutions, then it could be expected that they would develop policies which would favour their needs as opposed to the needs of corporate capitalism. Thus if the composition of the directorates of the World Bank and IMF were redrawn in favour of poorer nations then we could expect these institutions to develop policies in favour of the poorer countries. In particular we might expect them to be more lenient on the terms of debt repayment, or even to write off large chunks of debt accumulated over the past thirty years, as called for by prominent NGOs such as Jubilee 2000 and the World Development Movement. We might expect them to develop explicitly redistributionist policies encouraging developed countries to share with the developing world the patents and 'know-how' the lack of which hold the latter back from developing. We might expect them to be more generous about the degree to which states are able to finance welfare programmes, schools and health-care. In particular we could expect a challenge to the neoliberal insistence on markets in favour of strategies for development that are mindful of the very differing priorities and needs of countries across the developing world. The insistence on a rigged variant of 'free trade' in which the markets of the South are opened to the heavily state-subsidised goods of the North would, it could be expected, quickly be displaced by a variant of the 'fair trade' policies many NGOs and politicians in the South see as a necessity. 'Fair trade' would end the rigging of the market in favour of the North. It would prevent dumping, ensure that Northern producers rest within agreed norms of sustainable production and permit the unhampered flow of goods and services from South to North, thus making possible the 'trickle-down' effect described in Chapter 1.

Part of the assumption underpinning the demand for institutional reform is that the *role* of global bodies would change in perhaps radical ways. No longer would they be mere executors of the wishes of big business and the most powerful states; instead they would become arenas in which the diverse and plural needs of different states and regions would be able to be aired and acted upon. As properly 'political' bodies they would be open to diverse and plural conceptions of development, as opposed to development premised on the necessity for free markets, structural adjustment and cuts to public expenditure. The effect of such changes would be to narrow, if not cut completely, the 'democratic deficit' that currently allows the interests of the rich and powerful to dictate to the rest of the world how and under what terms economic development is to take place. It would lead to what Walden Bello of the NGO Focus on the Global South terms 'deglobalisation', meaning the displacement of the free market by a conception of managed development in the interests of the global poor. Whether such reforms would in fact result in the kind of radical rebalancing of the global economy depends in turn on certain propositions about the nature of the global political scene and elite behaviour more generally. These could be summarised as follows:

- the most powerful countries would continue to support financially global institutions that are no longer under their direct or indirect control, or which have priorities other than those that are supportive of their own industries. Global institutions were created by the global rich to serve the interests of the global rich. For them to serve the interests of the global poor, a massive shift in the values and behaviour of Northern elites is required, the like of which would be quite unprecedented in global politics. Up to the present the US has been notoriously lax in paying its UN bills. How much 'laxer' would US administrations become once power and influence shifted elsewhere – and particularly to the South?
- transnational capital will not be able to 'blackmail' reformed institutions into reintegrating their policies with the interests of transnational capital. Liberal internationalism puts its faith in the ability of institutions to exert influence over capital rather than vice-versa (as many argue is the case now). This would require at the very least a transformation of US and EU foreign policy away from the defence of 'national interests' towards a policy of 'enlightened' self-interest and a unilateral effort to cure the causes as well as the symptoms of global poverty.
- political elites in developing countries are prepared to risk confronting transnational capital in the name of some non-free

market model of economic development. One of the difficulties in the scenario envisaged here is that local and regional elites often ally themselves with the interests of capital, the US or both. This may be because they were put in power by the US or are maintained with the assistance of the US. Or it may reflect the desire of local elites to enrich themselves through acceptance of the 'assistance' offered by corporations. As postwar history illustrates, corruption of local elites is as much a *cause* of the South's miserable position as a symptom of it.

At the moment there has to be a question mark over all three assumptions about the prospects of institutional reform delivering substantive changes to the nature of economic globalisation. In particular it has to be questioned whether the US in its current 'mood' would be inclined to go along with institutions that no longer reflect its interests, or the interests of US-based corporations.

'strong(er)' reformism – or the return of social democracy

Milder variants of anti-capitalist reformism focus on institutions trusting that, with a change in the nature of global institutions, substantive outcomes will improve particularly for poorer countries. As is evident, such an approach may have radical implications both in terms of the composition and the role of current global institutions. *May* have. There is enough uncertainty about the effect institutional reform would have to suggest to many that a more radical approach is needed, one that in effect guarantees certain *outcomes* as well as a certain reconfiguration of those institutions. It is one thing to argue that political institutions need to be reformed and quite another to argue that certain outcomes or a certain redistribution of wealth is just or more equitable. Institutional reform may produce radical outcomes, but of course it may not. Radical or strong reformisms are underpinned by the uncertainty of a narrowly institutional approach, preferring instead to present a more or less ideologically driven vision of how global wealth and opportunity should be configured. Again, the details vary enormously between groups and activists, but what tends to inform this approach is the reinvigoration of what many commentators term 'social democracy'. Social democracy is a tradition of thought that dates back to the end of the nineteenth century. It is strongly associated with the organised labour movement and parliamentary labour parties that were created to defend the interests of working people. Today we hear social democratic demands being articulated by the International Confederation of Free Trade Unions (ICFTL), the Global Union Federations and the International Labour Organisation (ILO), as well as many well-known activists and intellectuals. What is perhaps novel about contemporary debates is that we find both those who favour a state-centred approach – aptly termed '*national internationalism*' – and others who favour a cosmopolitan approach with the object of a *global state* with global powers of redistribution. But we need, firstly, to get clear about what, broadly speaking, a social democratic approach amounts to.

'Social democracy' is a broad term that describes all those committed to making capitalism work for the interests of society generally, as opposed to the interests of big business and the well-off. Social democratic thought emerged initially as a critique of Marx's demand for the overthrow of the capitalist order and the private ownership of the means of production. Early social democratic theorists such as Eduard Bernstein argued that capitalism was not after all 'doomed' and that class polarisation would not cause its downfall. Socialists and progressives thus had to adopt a more 'evolutionary' approach to the task of developing a better society, using the productive energies unleashed by capitalist production to bring about more egalitarian policies. In this way they should nurture and promote capitalism's productive potential, whilst safeguarding the workers against the fluctuations of the 'trade cycle' and flagging demand. Capitalism would be 'milked' for the benefit of the thirsty masses, not just the capitalists themselves.

As social democratic thought developed in the early to mid-twentieth century, two considerations were uppermost in the thinking of social democrats in Europe. The first was the necessity for exercising *greater control over the market*, and the second was for *redistribution of resources* in accordance with some maxim of justice or equity. Control over the market was translated into 'demand-side economics', which is now associated with the work of the British economist John Maynard Keynes (hence 'Keynsianism'). It takes the view that the state has an *active* role to play in promoting capitalism and economic growth – as opposed to neoliberals who insist that only a passive or *laissez-faire* approach is appropriate. In particular the state should intervene to maintain 'demand', the key to maintaining that economic growth and productivity – without which, so it is held, modern societies would stagnate. Particularly in periods of economic down-swing, governments should borrow on the international money markets in order to invest in public works and public services, thereby providing the 'fuel' for continuing demand and the basis for economic recovery. In its more radical form (i.e. as 'democratic socialism'), social democracy translates into the belief in the necessity for 'socialistic' measures to complement private economic activity, as for example in the demand for the nationalisation of major industries or 'the commanding heights of the economy'. The idea is that the state can manage the economic affairs of its constituency, eliminating or minimising the severe fluctuations which are otherwise part of the trade cycle as well as the mass unemployment and hardship that accompanies it. The state should 'steer' the economy in ways that minimises the impact of recessions, whilst maximising the potential of the economy to return to full health and stability.

In terms of *redistribution*, an important part of the social democratic case is the belief that society will tolerate private ownership over the means of production if it is palpably of benefit to ordinary citizens. Economic growth is not in this sense to be considered an end in itself but rather a means to an end, which is the enrichment of society and the development of equality of opportunity, or more radically, (limited) equality of outcome. 'Equality of opportunity' is the belief that society should as much as possible eliminate factors preventing individuals from realising their full potential, such as poor housing, health or education. Equality of outcome additionally insists that the task of the state is to minimise – or even eliminate – the gap between the wealthiest and the poorest, thus necessitating very considerable state intervention. Social democracy thus enacts a kind of social *quid pro quo*. Business is able to get on with making money as long as in doing so it helps society and makes the lives of ordinary people, those who work for 'business', better. In turn business is furnished with a workforce that is better educated, healthier and thus is less likely to regard continuing inequalities as a reason to resist the *status quo*. Social democracy was (and still is) unembarrassed about being a kind of 'capitalism with a human face', a way in which the worst excesses of capitalist exploitation could be offset by socially progressive measures that benefited everyone. Now its relevance lies in terms of promoting a vision of globalisation 'with a human face' – for the benefit of the vast majority and not just for the 'fat cats' of the global North. But how is such a transformation to be effected?

social democracy as 'nationalist internationalism'

It is on this point that social democratically inclined elements of the anti-capitalist movement diverge. At the 2001 World Social Forum, for example, it was evident that the 'national internationalist' variant was in the ascendant. Here we can mention the platform of the Brazilian Workers Party (PT), hosts for the first three forums at Porto Alegre, and led by the charismatic President of Brazil, Lula da Silva. We can also mention those associated with the 'left republican' model of the strong state favoured by those allied in the context of French domestic politics to the '*bloc Chevènement*' and '*bloc Bourdieu*'. We can note that many trade unions, particularly in Europe and America, would regard a state-centred strategy as the best means of advancing towards a post-neoliberal global order, as would many domestic green parties and pro-peasant groups such as Bové's *Confédération Paysanne*. At the 2002 European Social Forum it was the demand for a strengthening of the state, particularly the institutions of the EU, that appeared to prevail in the plenary sessions. Why the state over global institutions?

The national internationalist position stems from the view that the nation-state remains the pre-eminent actor in global affairs, and potentially the primary site of resistance to global capital. Irrespective of the desirability or otherwise of a global state, the development of such a state is, it is argued a long way off. The nation-state is, however, still with us and can be mobilised to advance the cause of justice. As opposed to 'plain vanilla' nationalists, nationalist internationalists do not, however, argue for those old tools of national self-interest – protectionism and tariff barriers – to be re-erected (at least not in public). They are not, that is, calling for a return to the imperial if not colonial *status quo* in which the particular interests of wealthy nations rendered others subordinate. What they argue is that the best bulwark against untrammelled corporate power is for states to constrain the ability of transnational capitalists to move resources and production around the globe as they please. They point to the action taken, for example, by Malaysia to safeguard its economy in the wake of the 1997 Asian crisis. Refusing to stand mute before those who were scrabbling to shift their assets out of the country, Mohammed Mohathir imposed stiff penalties on the export of profits gained on the Kuala Lumpur stock exchange, a move which amazed many among the global elite for its sheer effrontery, yet which also gained a measure of grudging respect from the IMF. Speculators took notice, with the effect that Malaysia was spared the worst effects of the crisis even though it was still very badly hit. If, so the argument goes, states were to act together when setting common policies on taxation, on the terms and conditions under which companies can set up, and on labour policies, then business would be less inclined to move around to seek optimum conditions and would thus be less able to destabilise the efforts of states to set macro-economic policies in the interests of their citizens. In other words, states should act *together* to increase the costs associated with moving production, thereby undermining the mobility and liquidity of capital. This would safeguard the jobs and social investment which is part of the social democratic 'deal' for the citizens of individual nation-states. States need to bid each other *up* for the sake of keeping companies where they are, as opposed to bidding each other *down* (as they currently do) for the sake of attracting new capital as well as keeping companies already based in a given location.

The national state is moreover still the locus for social justice and for *redistribution* in accordance with nationally determined priorities. Again, 'national internationalists' are sceptical about the degree to which such priorities could be determined at global level when there is evidently such enormous disparity in terms of wealth, culture, and infrastructure between North and South. No global state could overcome such disparities or make them disappear. Thus the right to higher education enjoyed by, for example, French students would be meaningless in a context where the population lacks elementary education and is thus functionally illiterate. What countries in the North can and must do, however, is shift resources to the South so that development and opportunity follow.

One of the most imaginative suggestions of this kind is associated with the initiative launched by the ATTAC group (*Association pour la Taxation des Transactions Financiéres pour L'aide aux Citoyens* [Association for the Taxation of Financial Transactions to Aid Citizens]) created in France under the auspices of the journal *Le Monde Diplomatique* and responsible along with the PT for the establishment of the WSF. ATTAC is associated with high profile figures in the anti-capitalist movement such as Susan George,

Bernard Cassen and Ignatio Ramonet. ATTAC made headlines for picking up the suggestion associated with Nobel economist James Tobin that states should collect a tax on movements of capital, usually quoted as 0.1% of any transaction. The money collected would be used to fund projects in the developing world, thus shifting resources from wealthy banks and corporations to the global needy. Given the huge flows of money across the financial markets the sums involved are spectacular – as much as a billion dollars *a day* by some estimates. It is a difficult proposal to beat for its sheer simplicity and sheer immediacy. It also demonstrates clearly the nature of the national inter-nationalist variant of social democracy, which focuses on *using* capitalism for the benefit of the poor rather than *supplanting* capitalism with some other system of production. Rich countries need to club together to help poorer countries leading to greater stability and security, and in turn generating economic growth and greater equality of opportunity for all.

We still need to think, however, about the relationship of the national context to the international in 'nationalist international-ism'. What becomes apparent from the proposals is that the idea of the regional or continental bloc is an important part of the sugges-tion. Many leftists who support, for example, the idea of greater European integration do so on just such grounds, that is, because of the increased 'bargaining power' the EU has vis-à-vis transnational capital as opposed to any given nation-state acting alone. As a bloc composed of nearly 400 million citizens, with four out of the largest eight economies in the world on board, the EU can deploy consider-able muscle in its relations with capital. In particular it could ensure that the near-constant outflow of productive capacity to central and eastern Europe as well as Asia and Latin America experienced over the past three decades is stemmed before it empties the EU com-pletely of manufacturing. National internationalists argue that such moves cannot proceed on a unilateral basis. If they did then it would be little more than a form of Euro-nationalist protectionism. What is required rather is the development of analogous blocs elsewhere in the world. Thus they point to the potential of existing blocs such as MERCOSUR in Latin America or ASEAN in the Asia-Pacific region for providing a mutually supportive basis for such develop-ments. If there were blocs of this kind covering all the world regions then the freedom to roam of transnational capital would be severely circumscribed. Corporations would no longer be able to seek out the cheapest labour, but would have to negotiate with regional administrations over conditions of entry into the relevant area. Speculative flows could be monitored and taxed, minimum labour standards set and public-private initiatives delivered for the benefit of local populations. In such fashion capitalism would be used to serve the varying needs and interests of local blocs, thus creating stability as well as a degree of equality between different continents.

Again, we need to note that the credibility of such a position rests on certain key assumptions:

- Within regional or continental 'blocs' there needs to be enough common interest to maintain a 'united front' in the face of corporate attempts to seek out low cost manufacturing environments. This is less a problem for the EU, which is in any case bent on political as well as economic integration, but less obvious in the case of Asia, Africa or the Americas within which there is a great differentiation of wealth between countries. Poorer nations who may perceive the need for rapid inward investment in order to industrialise may be tempted to leave a bloc, perhaps temporarily, in order to increase inward investment vis-à-vis other members of the bloc.
- Similarly, at the global level there would have to be enough common interest to maintain a united front despite the massive inequalities between blocs and thus despite the considerable temptation 'low cost' blocs may have to attract inward investment by whatever means possible. What is the incentive for, say, a South Asian bloc to act in 'solidarity' with the European bloc so as to prevent the export of European jobs to India or Pakistan?
- The above in turn presupposes the availability of the political will as well as the ability to transfer massive resources from North to South in order to offset the effect of capital immobility and lack of investment. Presumably, Europeans and North Americans would be asked to subsidise the loss of inward investment experienced by less well-off blocs via some form of compensatory mechanism along the Tobin lines. How long would such a policy remain popular with voters? How long before mutuality led to protectionism?

The suggestion does not want for lack of wishful thinking. Those blocs that currently exist, such as the EU and ASEAN, arguably perform in exactly the opposite way to that intended. As 'national leftists and 'true' internationalists argue, the EU has so far imposed policies consonant with those of neoliberal orthodoxy, particularly as regards the necessity for balanced budgets, flexible labour markets, and reductions in social expenditure. Indeed the European Central Bank (ECB) has to date acted almost entirely in line with the strictures of the World Bank in imposing a deflationary regime orientated to generating economic growth at the cost of high levels of unemployment, a formula that could have been written by World Bank officials. Looking at the global picture, prospects are hardly more encouraging. There seems little incentive for low-cost or highly productive economies to go along with a bloc-built 'consensus' unless there is a massive compensatory mechanism to reassure them that they are not losing out. It would be interesting to hear the reactions of young people in Bulgaria, India or China, say, to the idea that what they need is *less* inward investment rather than more. How much compensation would have to be to paid to convince people who have been raised on a diet of 'trickle-down' economics, that there will be no 'trickle-down' after all – but only some sort of recompense for 'lost opportunity'? As NGOs like Forum for Global South fear, 'national internationalism' may become just a supranational 'nationalism'. This is particularly so where its advocates fail to show how a block on the movement of productive resources will aid those who currently look forward to the in-flow of resources caused by capital flight, the very phenomenon that encourages the wealthy to look to protectionist measures to defend their own workforce.

'we are the world': towards global social democracy

Arguably the most radical and certainly the most idealistic variant of reformism is that associated with the often heard demand for a 'world government' that would promote some form of 'global justice'. If not an explicit demand of many NGOs campaigning on issues to do with development, third world debt, environmental degradation and poverty, the demand for global social democracy is part of the 'background noise' of many of their policy documents and public announcements. This approach is also associated with many prominent academics and commentators on globalisation including David Held of the London School of Economics,

Richard Falk of Princeton, and George Monbiot a prominent British commentator and campaigner. To these groups and individuals the nation-state has already been surpassed as a locus of power, and thus as the site for any potential resistance to the encroachments of transnational capital. Many of them echo the concerns articulated briefly above, namely that any form of association or bloc beneath that of the world itself will fall prey to the ability of capital to play off competing interests against each other, thereby dragging states back into the game of 'beggar my neighbour'. What is required is concerted action at the *global* level, not merely to provide an institutional bulwark against the worst effects of capitalist globalisation, but an *alternative* model of economic globalisation, one that guarantees a certain minimum of security, justice and environmental protection for all, not just to those who luckily find themselves in an effective or wealthy 'bloc'. There are, it needs to be noted, many variants on the theme of global social democracy, but most of them share certain core ideas or concerns. These might be summarised in terms of the need to establish the *global management of economic affairs*; to enhance and augment *security*; to promote *justice and well-being*; to develop mechanisms of *accountability, representation and participation*; to foster the notion of '*global citizenship*'. Let's look briefly at the more significant elements.

In terms of economic affairs, social democrats look forward to the displacement of the free market by what might be termed a 'con-strained' market, that is a market in which capital is required to observe and obey certain basic principles, such as health and safety provision, pension and healthcare requirements, and holiday entitle-ments. More radical suggestions tend to emphasise the necessity for agreed universal minimum standards and rates of pay for every worker. Less radical demands emphasise the necessity to tailor pro-vision in accordance with local labour conditions, and prevailing rates of pay. In other words, less radical versions see the continuation of regional and local markets as inevitable, if not desirable. However all global social democrats agree that people should have access to certain minimum standards in terms of housing, sanitation, supply of clean water, and education. At the macro-economic level the sug-gestion is that public management would offset the worst effects of capitalist globalisation in terms of the massive in-flow and out-flow of assets and resources, as per the Asian economic crisis of 1997/8 and the Latin American crisis that followed immediately afterwards. Just as states currently work in partnership with companies to underwrite the costs and risks associated with development, so a global state would negotiate with corporations to ensure that the latter are not over-exposed in terms of the risks involved in setting up in the developing world. They envisage various forms of 'partnership' with transnational capital to ensure a proper trade off between risks and rewards for both business and the concerned workforce. What is uppermost is the desire to get away from the exploitative and demeaning 'sweatshop' conditions that much of the world's population currently endures.

Some globalisers further imagine a kind of global planning with decisions on economic management made in the sub-committees of a global parliament. As with national social democracy there is considerable variation in the degree to which activists and commentators see the management of macro-economic policy taking place. Some urge the 'Scandinavian' model of high corporate tax as the way to shackle business to the political agenda of a global government. Others see a 'French' style *dirigisme* with a significant planning element and control or even nationalisation of important or key industries as the only way to guarantee that companies would be made to obey their political masters. And of course there are many other models of social democracy available too, from the 'Rhineland' model of 'responsible' corporatism, to the British or 'Gaitskellite' (after the Labour politician) emphasis on increasing economic growth in the name of greater equality.

An imaginative recent proposal has recently been offered by George Monbiot in his *The Age of Consent*. It explicitly invokes Keynes's suggestions at the Bretton Woods negotiations in 1943/4 that set up the current international trading regime. Keynes argued for the establishment of a global bank or International Clearing Union (ICU) with its own currency, the 'Bancor'. Every state would be taxed on the basis of its trading balance with the bank on an annual basis. Countries falling into deficit would be charged interest on their 'account' and also required progressively to devalue their own currency. Countries running a surplus would be charged interest on their 'account' and made to raise the value of their currencies. What he envisaged, in short, was the use of fiscal instruments to assure a measure of redistribution from wealthy to poorer countries, together with incentives to prudence and greater investment across the developing world. It would ensure that the most successful trading countries were not allowed to exploit their position by, for example, maintaining a weak currency on international markets (such as the US has done). It would compel poorer countries to devalue, thereby making them more competitive whilst driving up productivity and the incentive to develop. In the Monbiot version this would be coupled with a regime of 'fair trade' in which protectionist measures and subsidies are outlawed except in the South (and then only for new industries). Inward investment would be hedged with restrictions with regard to environmental sustainability, minimum labour standards and health and safety provision. In common with other social democratic remedies, the key issue remains making global institutions accountable to the needs and interests of every state, not just the wealthy. It is also to ensure a managed and 'equitable' transfer of resources to the South: a true 'trickle-down' as opposed to the trickle-up relationship that arguably characterises current global trading patterns. Global capitalism must be made to serve the interests of the people, not the other way round.

As regards *social justice*, a global state would assure everyone a certain minimum standard of living. As in classical social democracy the means is through some form of global taxation system in which the global rich subsidise the global poor. This could be achieved either through taxation on global flows, such as in the ATTAC model discussed above, or through direct taxation of individual and corporate earnings. Nevertheless, the key point is to get the wealthy to pay for development programmes in the South. This would already be an advance on the *status quo* in which individuals and corporations may legally use off-shore havens and zero-tax areas to hide their wealth from the governments of nation-states. As globalisers point out, huge amounts of income are currently off-limits to governments, necessitating at least *some* form of global intervention to bring the wealthy to account. Many NGOs are, for example, currently urging some form of Marshall Plan to help the South. The Marshall Plan was proposed by the US in the immediate postwar period to the countries of Europe as a means of getting the European economies back on their feet and back into the global marketplace. The Plan was thus a form of enlightened self-interest which served the dual function of helping the needy, in this case the countries left devastated by war, and also helping the US which feared a lack of demand for its goods and services. The idea behind the contemporary Marshall Plan is the attempt to appeal to the same sense of enlightened self-interest shown by the US in 1947. Instead of confronting capital with a begging bowl, NGOs hope to appeal to the self-interest of Northern economies which look to expand consumption and boost production. Such a plan would be administered by global actors, perhaps foreshadowing greater partnership between the now burgeoning 'global civil society' and mechanisms of global governance. In any case, as many NGOs argue, without such mechanisms poor countries will sink further into the vicious circle of under-development, poverty and instability. Global governance on this reading is not some form of luxury, another layer of 'bureaucracy' to be paid for by the hard-pressed tax payers of the North. It is the only way in which massive and growing inequalities can be addressed in effective and immediate ways.

The same is true for *anti-monopoly mechanisms*, that is, mechanisms which prevent corporations establishing themselves as sole suppliers for goods and services and thus exploiting their position for immense gains, usually at the cost of the impoverished consumers of the developing world. The current campaigns against genetically modified goods and against the deployment of patents to generate immense profits for pharmaceutical companies trading on the HIV/Aids epidemic in Africa stem from such concerns. Again, they point to the need to beef up global regulation of corporations to bring an end to the exploitation of those who are ill-equipped to fight back.

This highlights the necessity for global institutions to promote *security and democratic governance* against the onslaught of 'predatory' globalisation. In terms of security, an unfettered free market is regarded as the economic analogue of a political 'free-for-all' or state of nature in which the strongest always win, usually at the cost of the common good. Pollution and environmental degradation are persistent themes, with globalists maintaining that without properly constituted global protocols – and the means of implementing them – the rich can always 'opt out' of agreements to suit their own selfish needs, usually to the detriment of the less well-off. But, as recent history shows, sometimes countries in the developing world are their own worst enemies, and they need to be encouraged to work within stable and universally agreed norms in order not to degrade their own environments in the haste to meet their own population's ever-expanding needs. Again, social democrats argue that only a global regulatory framework would be able to make both rich and poor sign up to green policies, safeguarding the interests of the global 'commons'.

Security concerns often have a wider orbit as well in social democratic demands, encompassing the need for strengthened control on arms proliferation which again is often sponsored or underwritten by wealthy nations of the North keen to sell the latest weapons and gadgets to governments in the developing world who are worried about threats from neighbours, themselves armed by western companies. A system of *global conflict management* would, so it is argued, help reduce regional and local rivalries, thereby diminishing the fear of armed force and permitting an open dialogue between countries that have sometimes been goaded on by wealthier on-lookers seeking to support their arms industries. A system based on nation-states is one likely to maintain insecurity and the need for armaments. A system of global governance and universal mediation is likely to reduce global tensions and would promote much needed expenditure on welfare and social security. Similarly, global governance would, it is anticipated, institutionalise a global dialogue of the kind that has been singularly lacking throughout the history of the modern world, yet which is needed to underpin the rights of minorities and cultural diversity. Without such a system, diversity is regarded as a threat, a 'clash of civilisations' between irreconcilable cultural forces. Here is an echo of the Kantian theme touched on above of the desirability and indeed necessity for humanity to reconcile itself to co-existence and co-operation. Without it, so the argument goes, the world will forever remain hostage to those with economic, as well as perhaps cultural and religious, reasons for promoting antagonism and conflict. To social democrats the best means of avoiding such an outcome is the institutionalisation of dialogue and the elaboration of rights that protect and promote 'difference', however constituted.

Finally, strong reformists tend to agree with the weaker, institutionalist variant on the need for the democratisation of global institutions and the development of an ethic and practice of *global citizenship*. The issue of the democratic deficit looms large once again, with many critics and activists voicing their concern about the lack of accountability, representation and opportunities to participate at the global level. The existence of a global civil society, of different groups, NGOs, and other-non-state actors is testament, so it is claimed, to the existence of a global constituency and thus of the need for institutions and procedures in which the constituency can be heard. Here however, opinion again divides. Milder variants tend to focus on the 'immediate' need for the formalisation of representation for NGOs and particular interests in existing institutions, such as the UN and the WTO. This is to say that 'global civil society' (i.e. NGOs) should be 'listened to' or, better, represented in existing structures of decision-making. More robust variants stress the necessity for wholesale changes to the system of governance, permitting the development of a global state proper perhaps through an extension of the UN, with directly or indirectly elected parliamentary chambers and global elections for global parties. This would be a 'globalisation' of the form of representative democracy we find in social democratic states with perhaps increased safeguards for the rights of minorities, mechanisms for rendering both private and public actors accountable, funding for 'global' lobbyists and access to the global media. There are many variants on the theme, reflecting the many variants of representative democracy available around the globe. However, certain themes tend to stand out in such schemes, for example:

- the necessity for *'multi-level governance'*, meaning systems in which decisions can be taken at the appropriate level (sub-national, national, regional, continental, global) or in consultation with the appropriate constituency (developing countries, agricultural regions, areas experiencing famine, religious minorities). Few in other words argue for a unitary or UK-style state with a powerful centralised authority, but rather a heavily tiered representative system fully embracing 'subsidiarity' – the principle that decision-making is made by representatives at the level nearest to those affected by the outcome.
- the need for *transparency and accountability*. Those who govern should be subject to rigorous checks from 'below' whether by parliamentary committee, the media or other 'constituents'. This would be in contrast with the secretive or heavily veiled meetings of global institutions like the IMF and the WTO where most of the business is conducted in the 'green room', i.e. in private.
- the need for *sensitivity to cultural diversity, tradition, and the rights of minority groups and peoples*. A necessary feature of any progressive equivalent of global structures would be to make them responsive to the very different needs and values of the world's populations. This points to constitutional safeguards for religious practices, minority media outlets, multilingual structures.

In short, the social democratic concern with 'who gets what, how and when?' needs to be augmented by the contemporary liberal concern to ensure parity of treatment, a secure or constitutionally based system of human rights and possibly 'group' rights. It also needs to be complemented with the 'green' concern to provide a basis for sustainable development or patterns of economic activity that are less damaging than the more or less unfettered market system we have at present. 'Citizenship' must in this sense not only be genuinely global, but genuinely inclusive of those who might otherwise be excluded. In short, social democracy would have to be genuinely universalist whilst paying great attention to the needs and interests of the very many minorities, groups, nations and peoples that compose the 'globe'.

could global social democracy work – for whom?

Defenders of a social democratic approach, whether weakly or strongly ideologically based, consider themselves 'realists' in the sense that often their arguments are framed with a view to countering or challenging those further to the left than themselves. This reflects the origins of social democracy as an alternative to revolutionary socialisms generally and Marxism in particular. It is probably true to say that on these terms it is indeed more realistic, if only in the sense that it asks quite a lot less of elites than do Marxists or other revolutionary groups. It proposes to *ask* global elites to give up some of their power and privilege rather than to *divest* them of it, as is implied in radical approaches. Nonetheless, viewed from the perspective of the present, even a social democratic programme looks uncompromisingly 'radical' from the point of view of the 'wild frontier' of global capitalism. This is particularly so viewed from the position of the US which, virtually alone among the advanced capitalist countries, has little in the way of a social democratic tradition to draw on to make the comparison. This is a particularly important point in that it is noticeable that the argument for global social democracy tends to work by *analogy*. What this means is that those who advocate social democratic measures rely on transferring an argument that has enjoyed widespread validity at the national level to the global level. To take an example from contemporary Britain, we frequently hear the complaint that health-care is better in some important respect in one part of the country immediately followed by the demand that the situation be remedied. Don't we all pay our taxes? Don't we all in this sense have a right to the same level of health-care? What we rarely hear by way of a reply is that people in one part of Britain pay proportionately far more in taxes than do those in some other poorer part, and so should have access to better health-care. In this sense health issues in the UK are still dominated by a social democratic discourse that insists on equality of access and equality of services, *irrespective* of the ratio of payment either individually or at local or regional level. 'Citizenship' in such a context implies equality of access to resources provided by the state no matter where one finds oneself.

What global social democrats hope is that just as most people in the UK do not query the right of people to right of equal health-care, so they will not query the right of people across the world to, if not equal health-care, then let's say some *adequate* health-care (relative to some internationally agreed norm). What they hope is that just as we accept certain obligations towards our fellow citizens here, so we will accept certain obligations to everyone. We will come (or are coming) to see the population of the world as in some way analogous to the way citizens in social democratic countries view their fellow citizens: not just as 'consumers' or 'workers' or capitalists, but as people with particular needs which it is our duty to help satisfy. This is what it means to live in a civilised society; this is what it *should* mean to live in a civilised world.

It is a noble sentiment, but one that many would argue is actually in relative decline where it once existed, and a far-off 'communitarian' ideal in countries where it never existed. As writers such as Robert Puttnam and Zygmunt Bauman lament, the tendency of modernisation is towards greater *individualisation* rather than the generation of greater community spirit. If such commentators are to be believed, we as modern citizens increasingly lack 'social capital'. We lack that stock of associations and bonds that takes us out of our otherwise solitary existences and places us in a social context where we can see how important we are to others and in turn how important others are for the realisation of our goals and aspirations. Thus according to the relevant data we increasingly resent the community or social obligations we are said to owe to others. We don't like paying taxes, particularly when those taxes are used to fund services for particular groups, causes or minorities with whom we ourselves feel little sympathy.

So much for the bleak prognostications of academic research. It is probably true that the effort to generate genuinely global sentiments represents an idealistic gesture of Herculean proportions. But what global social democrats can point to is that if globalisation has had one effect in the cultural domain then it is in terms of the increased awareness of our proximity to others. The term 'global village' is an awful cliché; but it is one that nonetheless speaks to an important aspect of contemporary consciousness. People are getting 'nearer' to each other: nearer in terms of the time it takes to communicate with others across the globe, nearer in terms of time to get *to* other parts of the world, nearer in terms of the lag between events occurring and their appearing on our TV screens. But we are also forced to be 'near' in terms of global political problems: environmental degradation, international conflict, poverty caused by international trade agreements. 'Nearness' (or 'proximity') is for social democrats a key factor in thinking about who is 'relevant' to our lives, to whom we feel a duty of care, to whom we feel some sense of solidarity. In some important sense today's social democrats share with the social democrats of the late nineteenth century the view that we *do* care in some way for those who are near, and also that we *should* care for those who are near. Today, everyone is 'near'. Our obligations are therefore universal rather than regional, national or local.

Before leaving the subject it is however important to consider the means by which this vision is set to become a reality. As we mentioned above, social democrats have historically regarded themselves as 'realists', particularly when set alongside those we shall shortly consider. Yet the grounds of social democratic 'realism' was much more apparent than now in the cases of the welfare states they helped develop a century ago. Social democracy prospered because it was able to take advantage of the development of universal suffrage across Europe in the nineteenth and early twentieth century. By appealing to the interests of the newly enfranchised, social democrats were able to utilise the collective power of the 'masses' to further policies of social justice and demand management. The difficulty with transferring the social democratic analogy across to the contemporary situation is that there is no global 'state' to speak of, nor much of a prospect of one being created given the powerful forces lined up to ensure that such a state remains a pipedream. This underlines the degree to which the call for global social democratic measures is itself a radical – even utopian – one rather than a 'realistic' one under contemporary conditions. Indeed, the global social democrats find themselves in the position of the Jacobins rather than the Victorian 'progressives' they sometimes sound like. Like the former they need to create 'political authority' first, and *then* attempt to deploy it for whatever egalitarian and redistributive measures it is agreed should be pursued. Whether this can be done 'politely', that is, without holding a gun to the heads of global elites – for example through the threat of withholding debt repayments as advocated by Monbiot – is a matter for intense debate both within and without 'reformist' circles.

resources

read on

Zygmunt Bauman, *The Individualized Society* (Oxford: Polity Press, 2001).

Walden Bello, *De-Globalization: Ideas for a New World Economy* (London: Zed Books, 2003).

Tony Blair, 'Doctrine of the International Community', April 1999, www.number-10.gov.uk/output/Page1297.asp

Pierre Bourdieu, *Acts of Resistance: Against the New Myths of Our Time* (Cambridge: Polity Press, 1998).

José Bové, *The World is Not for Sale: Farmers Against Junkfood* (London and New York: Verso, 2002).

Bill Clinton, 'The Struggle for the Soul of the Twenty-First Century' (BBC Richard Dimbleby Lecture, December 2001), www.clintonpresidentialcenter.com/dimbleby.html

Richard Falk, *Predatory Globalization: A Critique* (Oxford: Polity Press, 1999).

Liza Featherstone, *Students Against Sweatshops: The Making of a Movement* (London and New York: Verso, 2000).

Susan George, *The Lugano Report: On Preserving Capitalism in the Twenty First Century* (London: Pluto, 1999).

Anthony Giddens, *The Third Way* (Cambridge: Polity Press, 1999).

John Gray, *False Dawn* (London: Granta, 1998).

David Held et al., *Global Transformations: Politics, Economics and Culture* (Cambridge: Polity Press, 1999).

Will Hutton, *The World We're In* (London: Little Brown, 2002).

Immanuel Kant, *Perpetual Peace* [1795], various editions. Full text available online at: www.constitution.org/kant/perpeace.htm

George Monbiot, *The Age of Consent* (London: Flamingo, 2003).
Robert Puttnam, *Bowling Alone: The Collapse and Revival of American Community* (New York: Simon & Schuster, 2001).
Jan-Aart Scholte, *Globalization: A Critical Introduction* (London: Macmillan, 2000).
George Soros, *Open Society* (London: Little Brown, 2000).

link to

www.nosweat.org.uk
www.nosweatapparel.com
www.jubilee2000uk.org
www.wdm.org.uk (World Development Movement)
www.oxfam.org
www.focusweb.org (Focus on the Global South)
www.icftu.org (International Confederation of free Trade Unions)
www.ilo.org (International Labour Organization)
www.confederationpaysanne.fr
www.mondediplo.com (English language edition of *Le Monde Diplomatique*)
www.attac.org
www.forumsocialmundial.org.br (World Social Forum)

a 'movement of movements'

ii: renegades, radicals and revolutionaries

In the last chapter we considered the 'anti-capitalism' of the reformers: an anti-capitalism that is 'anti-corporate power', 'anti-neoliberal' or 'anti-the-free-market' but not anti-capitalist on a strict reading of the term. They do not call for the abolition of the private ownership of the means of production, an end to 'wage labour' or to production for profit, as opposed to some other principle. This is not to say that reformist anti-capitalisms are not themselves 'radical'. As we discussed, under current conditions most schemas that stray from acceptance of the market and the neoliberal agendas of global institutions have a perhaps undeniably 'radical' air to them. Nevertheless, they call for a modification of global capitalism, not its elimination or transformation. In Part Two of our analysis of the 'movement of movements' we look at those who *are* in some fundamental respect anti-capitalist on these terms. In particular we need to cover the three main radical groupings *Marxist and neo-Marxist* groupings, *anarchism* and radical *environmentalism*. By way of a contrast to these more or less ideologically driven positions we also look at '*Zapatismo*', the ideas and analysis of the Zapatistas and Subcomandante Marcos.

marxism after the 'fall of communism'

It may come as a surprise after all we have said about the death of Marxism or communism in chapter two, to begin a consideration of the radical wing of anti-capitalism with Marxist groups. If Marxism is 'dead', why are we looking at it? Attentive readers of the relevant chapter will have noted that one of the key distinctions drawn in the exposition was between official and unofficial politics, that is between national politics, the politics of electioneering, political parties and voting, and the subterranean 'unofficial' politics that began to proliferate after 1968. What we noted there was that 'official Marxism' – the Marxism of the Communist Bloc – went into decline after that point and eventually succumbed in all but a handful of countries after the Fall of the Wall in 1989. China, the most powerful of the remaining 'Marxist' regimes, appears increasingly embarrassed about its Marxist-Leninist heritage, and rightly so given its enthusiasm for quasi-capitalist forms of production. On the other hand, 'unofficial' Marxism – the Marxism that vehemently *criticised* the Soviet Union, the Communist Bloc as well as the West – has never gone away. Indeed as is evident, Marxist groups have been amongst the most important and most visible at anti-capitalist protests, particularly in Europe. Marxist writers such as Alex Callinicos and Daniel Bensaid have offered analyses of the meaning of the anti-capitalist phenomenon as well as prescribing programmes and strategies for the anti-capitalist resistance. Many Marxist groups are well-organised and well-furnished with the means of making their presence felt, whether it be in the preparation of banners and placards, in the printing of posters, leaflets and newspapers, or in organising carnivals, festivals, summer schools and teach-ins. Marxists are also prominent on the organising committees of anti-capitalist protests and umbrella groups. The website of 'Globalise Resistance', one of the better known activist networks in the UK, reports that eleven out of twenty-six of its steering committee are members of Marxist groupings, predominantly the SWP.

Yet at the same time, to suggest that the relative success of Marxist groups in attaining prominence in the anti-capitalist movement is simply due to superior organisation and resources, is to ignore the central fact about Marxism. This is that the works of Marx offer the oldest, most sophisticated and most complete account of capitalism and its travails. Marxism offers a critique of capitalism in all its dimensions, ethical, moral, political and economic. It also offers a ready account of what it is that should replace capitalism, and offers some indications of how to get there. None of which is to say that what Marx wrote has to be regarded as compelling, convincing or indeed 'correct' in some relative or absolute sense. As we shall see, there are many radicals within the anti-capitalist movement who argue that not only is Marx in some important sense 'wrong', but also that Marxism is a pernicious and harmful 'doctrine' that has to be isolated and combated wherever possible. Nonetheless it is also a truism to note that Marxism is *one* of the most, if not *the* most, important currents of contemporary anti-capitalism and merits consideration on these terms alone. It also merits consideration in the sense that getting clear about what Marxism offers will help us to get clear about the two other principle radicalisms of the anti-capitalist movement, anarchism and environmentalism, as well as the many hybrid positions between them, and indeed Zapatismo.

Anyone who has been on anti-capitalist demonstrations or who has followed the fortunes of radical politics in the run-up to Seattle will know that that there are literally hundreds of Marxist groups or groupuscules around the world. Their names generally contain at least two of the following terms: 'Marxist' (and/or-'Leninist'), 'socialist'/'communist', 'people's'/'workers', 'party'/'movement'/ 'tendency', 'international', 'revolutionary' and 'popular'. Sometimes the name of the relevant 'host' country is appended, helpfully making clear the point of origin of the particular group in question. Some of these groups are tiny, no more than a handful of hardy souls producing a newsletter or leaflet. Others are much larger. The UK Socialist Worker Party (SWP) claims to have at least 10,000 members, and, given recent developments, this may not be an exaggeration. There are significant Marxist groupings in Italy, the United States and France. Indeed Marxist or quasi-Marxist parties polled nearly 15% of the popular vote in the French presidential election of 2002. Marxism remains an important current in Greek and Turkish politics, in the politics of many Asian countries such as India, and also in Latin America and South Africa. Indeed, the only places with little or no Marxist activity are the former Communist states, where unsurprisingly anything associated with the old order is often looked upon with disdain, particularly by younger people. Nonetheless the appeal of Marxism to *activists* is significant, and it is easy to see why.

Firstly, Marxism offers an intellectually coherent and highly sophisticated analysis of capitalism, one that like all great doctrines stems from an essentially simple idea: that capitalist production represents a form of exploitation. Capitalism 'begins' by appropriating the basic resources that we require to live an independent existence, particularly the land taken over in the global process of 'primitive capitalist accumulation'. Having dispossessed people of the land,

capitalists then exploit those without the means of their own subsistence (i.e. the working class), paying them a fraction of the value
they produce and keeping the rest as profits. Yet the critique of capitalism is not *merely* moral or ethical in nature, as it is for certain
strands of anarchism and socialism, but one based on the certainty
that capitalism is unsustainable in the long term. It is also based on a
particular conception of rationality and human progress that insists
on the *necessity* for capitalism as a prelude to the construction of
'higher' forms of social life. This illustrates an important fact about
Marx's work, which is that he believed that without modernisation,
industrialisation and the wholesale transformation of life that goes
along with it, there could be no socialism, let alone communism.
Marx was in this sense a creature of the Enlightenment. Whilst he
was deeply pained by the spectacle of capitalist production, he was a
great admirer of the advances made under capitalism in the field of
production. What angered him was that production was for profit
rather than the satisfaction of human needs. The right of 'private
property' was a right enjoyed by the few, not the many. Capitalism
had in this sense prepared the way for a higher form of existence, but
was itself the obstacle to its realisation. It thus had to be overthrown
by the class that capitalism itself creates, namely the 'proletariat' or
working class.

Even on the basis of this minimal description we can glean certain important facts about Marxist approaches to resistance and the
nature of the post-capitalist order to come. Firstly, Marx looked to
the working class to be the agent of change. At one level this was simply because he thought that the tendency of capitalist production
was to reduce the number of classes to two, namely the proletariat
and the bourgeoisie. But on another it was because he thought that
what made people potentially revolutionary was the *experience* of
being exploited or alienated. Intellectuals like himself could
empathise with labour, but historically they were just as likely, if not
more so, to side with the owners. For workers, who actually experienced increased competition and exploitation, there was little
choice. It was fight back or succumb to a life of servitude and
squalor. Marx also saw that advanced production, particularly factory production, made for a different kind of individual, one used to
working *collectively*. Working together gave people the impetus to
act together against a common enemy and in a common cause.
These and other factors made him invest his hopes and expectations
in the proletariat.

Secondly, it is important to note that Marx was a communist, not a socialist. He considered socialism a stage *on the way to* communism. This is to say that he looked forward to the *complete* abolition of private property, of classes, of fundamental distinctions between peoples, nations, individuals. He also looked forward to the complete abolition of the state, the police, the judicial apparatus and everything else that went with it. If this sounds like Marx was an anarchist, then we should point out that the First International, created in 1864, included anarchists as well as communists and socialists, the distinctions being perhaps less sharp then than they are now. Marx *was* a kind of anarchist. Indeed he often accused his anarchist opponents such as Pierre-Joseph Proudhon and Mikhail Bakunin of not being consistent in their opposition to the state. But his 'anarchism' involved, paradoxically, a great deal of organisation, too much for his anarchist critics. This is a reasonable point. Marx wanted *both* a highly advanced, highly industrialised form of life, one that surrendered nothing in its progress towards a better world; but he also wanted individuals to be fully involved in all the decisions affecting them. He thought planning offered the best means of ordering an economy (as he made clear in *The Communist Manifesto*); but he also looked forward to the *complete* decentralisation of decision-making as described in his sympathetic portrayal of the Paris Commune of 1871. He wanted the individual to develop all her potential, to become 'many-sided', but he *also* wanted her to feel at one with the collective. He wanted the proletariat to emancipate itself, but he also wrote in terms of the necessity for the Communist Party to show the proletariat 'the line of march', thereby implying that it could not emancipate itself without the help of intellectuals and the 'most advanced' sections of the class organised above and beyond the 'less' advanced.

the (many) sons and daughters of marx

The above points give us a clue as to why there are so many competing Marxisms on offer, with so many different groups and parties all jostling for our attention. Some groups emphasise the need for planning; others the need for local or decentralised decision-making. Some stress the necessity for the party or movement to 'lead'; others stress the capacity of ordinary people for self-organisation. Some stress Marx's attachment to a strict historical 'timetable', inferring that revolution can only be legitimate at a certain point of historical development; others stress the 'contingent' or self-determining nature of Marx's work, implying that revolution will occur whenever ordinary people, as opposed to economic indicators, say it is 'ready'. Some think that all these different aspects of Marx's approach can be integrated into a non-contradictory and perfectly consistent whole. The point is, none of these interpretations is 'wrong', because all of them can be found in some corner or other of Marx's vast opus. And if they cannot be found there, then they can be found in one of Marx's authoritative followers such as Lenin or Trotsky, or Gramsci or whomever.

This in turn illustrates what is particularly distinct about Marxism as a politics: it relies very heavily on *the use and interpretation of texts,* not just those of Marx, but also of Marx's followers. Marxist groupings seek to develop a 'line' on all the key issues of the day, and this is informed by a continual reading and rereading of works by Marx and his followers. In this sense asking why there are so many Marxisms is akin to asking why there are so many different Christian churches and sects. Where doctrines rely on the interpretation of texts one is almost bound to have schism, particularly where there are *so many* texts. There is only one Bible (or two testaments), but the *Collected Works of Marx and Engels* (aptly shortened to the 'MEGA') run to fifty volumes at the last count. The further point is that whilst Marx *was* a remarkably consistent thinker, he was also a remarkably flexible one, or, to put it less charitably, he could say something on one occasion and appear to contradict himself on another. This is fun for scholars of Marx to pick over, but politically it means that there is a continual sparring between and amongst Marxists on certain crucial issues, like the role of the party, or the exact nature of the 'transition' between capitalism and communism, the exact moment when revolution becomes legitimate. As a result there is not one 'Marx', but lots of Marxs, and we can add lots of Lenins and Trotskys too.

But isn't there something, some essential core to Marxism that will help the beginner decide if and to what degree it holds anything of any use to him or her? Here we need to be brave and suggest the following as a 'rough guide' to what Marxism means as a variety of anti-capitalism.

- *the primacy of productive processes and thus of class struggle for 'reading' anti-capitalism.* Other kinds of struggle, for example, for human rights or environmental measures are all in some sense 'secondary' and thus subordinate to economic considerations 'in the final analysis'. They are symptoms of capitalist oppression, and thus can only be alleviated by overthrowing capitalism itself. This helps explain why Marxists get accused of 'cynicism' in their relations with groups who see the latter as reducing all oppressions to one: that of the working class.

- *the necessity of working class organisation for defeating capitalism.* Only the working class, acting *as a class* has the power to defeat capitalism. This is because it is only the withdrawal of labour that really damages the capitalist class, particularly as, on a Marxist reading, it is labour that creates value for the capitalist. From this point of view Marxists utterly reject the view described in chapter two that the working class is 'dead' or irrelevant to an anti-capitalist movement.

- *necessity for a party or movement to oversee the revolutionary process and initiate measures needed to begin the transition to communism.* To be successful a revolutionary assault on capitalism requires organisation, planning, strategy, tactics. All this implies the necessity for self-organisation via a party or movement with a leadership which is able to prosecute its aims and objectives.

- *transfer of the means of production into the hands of the workers* (or those representing their interests). Ultimately 'anti-capitalism' is about the reappropriation of the productive resources of the world for humanity as a whole. This may involve bloodshed, but in Marx's view need not necessarily do so. Indeed, he was happy in his own writings to tinker with more or less 'gradual' ways in which to transfer the productive wealth of the few into the hands of society through nationalisation, joint stock companies and the like.

- *socialism is a transitionary stage on the way to communism.* Socialism can never be considered an end in itself. Communism is the *complete* abolition of private property and the market. Distribution of goods should be in accordance with 'needs', not 'work', let alone any market-derived formula. Marx was an avowed *critic* of socialist and social democratic notions of 'egalitarianism' and 'distributive justice'.

Compared with the positions we have described so far this is a radicalism of a spectacularly uncompromising kind. What Marx offered *was* a glorious vision, one moreover that helped inspire many of the 'anti-capitalist' revolutions of the twentieth century. Yet critics argue that this same vision was used to justify the indescribable cruelties of the early Soviet period: War Communism, the putting down of the Kronstadt rebellion, and the genocidal lunacy of the Gulag. This is to say nothing of the Cultural Revolution and the various massacres conducted by 'Marxists' in the course of the previous century. It is the 'glorious' vision that maintains the allegiance and energies of contemporary Marxist groups. It is the memory of the various attempts to enact the vision – as well as for some the vision itself – that sustains the equally vociferous critique of Marxism from its ideological and political opponents – as we shall see.

beyond 'bolshevism': autonomism, council communism and 'heterodox' radicalism

Notwithstanding the above discussion, it needs to be asserted that Marxism can be more or less ideological as we are using the term here. This is to say that there are Marxists who are stubbornly 'doctrinal' in their approach, holding that there is only one 'correct' version of Marx's work, only one 'correct' vision of how anti-capitalism might develop as a movement, and only one correct view of what a post-capitalist society could be like. Sectarianism is and always has been endemic in Marxist circles for precisely this reason. It is certainly not limited to the Bolsheviks – the Party of Lenin, Trotsky and Stalin which gave us the term 'Bolshevism' – which nowadays tends to be used more as a term of abuse, i.e. to describe those for whom fealty to 'the line', the Party and centralised 'discipline' have become ends in themselves.

Yet there are also Marxists (and revolutionary socialists) who are much less committed to maintaining a doctrinal or ideological 'line' in this sense and thus more willing to regard the process of revolutionary struggle as one involving working class *self*-organisation and *self*-understanding. Chief amongst these would be the various 'autonomist' or non-Leninist Marxisms. Some of these date back to the earliest years of the Russian Revolution and the failure of the Bolsheviks to deliver the 'soviet' democracy promised by Lenin on coming to power. In this sense autonomist Marxism was a direct challenge to Bolshevism and to the idea of the Soviet Union as the locus for 'anti-capitalist' initiatives. Early 'council communists' such as Anton Pannekoek, Paul Mattick and Karl Korsch focused particularly on the possibilities inherent in the soviet's or workers' councils as a basis for social organisation. They stressed the need for decentralisation of decision-making, a high degree of communal or cantonal autonomy and thus the need for vigilance against the encroachments of the state and large-scale bureaucracy of the sort developing in the Soviet Union. They also stressed the necessity for a consensual basis for revolutionary transformation and thus again the need to recognise and permit differences between communes and collectives. Autonomist Marxism received a major boost in 1968, particularly in France where the Situationist critique, looked at briefly in chapter two, accelerated the rejection of traditional party structures by many leftists.

As regards developments post-68, the currency of autonomist ideas and themes is pervasive, particularly in Italy which, with Germany and Holland, has a strong autonomist tradition in thought and action. All three have significant networks of autonomists in major cities with extensive activities, support groups, established facilities for squatters, lobby groups, and micro-economic structures. Indeed, so extensive are such networks in certain cities that it is little exaggeration to describe them as parallel societies operating outside 'mainstream' society. In terms of distinct groupings perhaps the highest profile 'autonomist' network would be *Ya Basta!* (Enough!) formed after 1994 in solidarity with the Zapatista rebellion. Along with the *Tuti Bianchi* and the WOMBLES (or 'White Overalls Movement Building Libertarian Effective Struggles'), they have been a colourful presence at the larger anti-capitalist demonstrations. Elsewhere there are a huge number of autonomist collectives, groupuscules and affinity groups, including those associated with journals and newsletters such as *Fifth Estate, Aufhebung* and *Midnight Notes*. We can also mention the innumerable currents, collectives and communes sympathetic to the work of intellectuals such as Deleuze, Guattari, Hakim Bey, Toni Negri and Mario Tronti. One of the more significant theoretical works to appear since Seattle, *Empire* written by Negri and Michael Hardt, is imbued with the *spirit* of autonomism, even if its actual recommendations fall curiously short of the radical measures many identifying with autonomism would associate with it. Given this diversity of autonomist perspectives it would stretch matters to talk about an autonomist 'movement' as such. Indeed, as will be evident looking at their publications and websites, there is as much bickering about 'correct' interpretations of key thinkers and theories amongst autonomist factions as there is within Marxism, even if relations between autonomist groups seem less sour than between Marxist groups. Nonetheless it is evident that 'autonomism' is a key current of contemporary anti-capitalist resistance and so needs to be thought about further. So how could we summarise what it stands for as a tradition of thought and action?

- Autonomism and its various currents such as 'Operaism' stress the 'open' nature of the historical process and thus the *importance of political struggle over economic forces*. Indeed certain variants of autonomism would assert that economic forces are themselves determined by class struggles, thereby reversing the line developed by many of Marx's 'orthodox' followers. The significance of such a move theoretically, is that it leads to an 'open' account of how resistance to capitalism arises, and thus to a less doctrinaire account of who as well as what can be considered 'progressive' from the point of view of developing an anti-capitalist resistance. Thus autonomists are interested in supporting and developing struggles wherever and however they arise.
- Autonomism has an open stance on the question of who or what is to be considered '*working class*'. Whereas Leninists have tended to favour the industrial proletariat, autonomists have regarded 'class composition' as a more complex matter. On some readings, students and housewives could be regarded as 'working class', particularly where such groups have joined in more general struggles for social and economic improvements.
- This leads, thirdly, to a *flexible stance on the nature of an anti-capitalist resistance* and its possible outcomes. Autonomists argue that it is the concentration of political and economic power that has to be combated, whether this power be in the hands of the capitalist class or 'representatives' of the working class itself such as trade union leaderships or communist party bosses. If not post-ideological as such, the stress on the self-organisation of ordinary people leads many autonomists to accept, indeed, celebrate the idea of multiple 'post-capitalisms', different visions of how the world can look.
- Historically, autonomism has favoured *decentralisation* and '*localisation*' over a transitory dictatorship of the proletariat subordinating local struggles to one-arching state form. Any

future society must be one based on communal autonomy, not the state.

In this sense autonomism stresses the facility ordinary people have for developing appropriate structures and forms of decision-making for themselves. This echoes the roots of the early (radical) critique of Bolshevism, which saw the latter as subordinating such forms of self-organisation to the needs of a vanguard party standing outside or beyond the working class itself. Autonomism might be thought of, then, as one way in which Marxism could be rendered in a less ideologically rigidified form.

anarchism, or the art of not being 'in charge'

In the early nineteenth century revolutionaries and radicals of many different kinds were found under the same umbrella, namely The International Working Men's Association, otherwise known as the First International. It was set up in 1864 to coordinate working class resistance and the activities of various affiliated groups and parties. Marx, who quickly became the leading light of the International, envisaged it becoming a political party and a basis for securing power for the working class. This brought him into conflict with the many anarchists who were also involved in the International, many of whom followed Bakunin's critique of 'organised politics' of the sort demanded by Marx. Rupture followed. Bakunin and many other anarchists from the International were expelled (or left) and anarchism and Marxism became the irreconcilable factions we see today. Although it is easily assumed that Marxism must be the more significant tendency, not least because of the 'success' of Marxist groups in capturing power in a number of countries, anarchism too has been a serious force in revolutionary and anti-capitalist politics. It has been capable of mobilising huge numbers despite – or perhaps because of – its 'lack' of a developed ideology of the sort associated with Marxism. Anarchists were a major presence in the rebellions and uprisings of the late nineteenth and early twentieth centuries, particularly in Europe and Latin America. Anarchists were very much to the fore in the Russian Revolution and indeed helped establish Soviet power in the early years of the new regime. Once the 'libertarian' goals of the Revolution were 'betrayed', anarchist leaders such as Nestor Makhno succeeded in capturing and controlling large tracts of land from both the Bolsheviks and the counter-revolutionary White forces, proving a major thorn in the side to both. The high tide of anarchism as a political force was reached in the Spanish Civil War when the anarchists were perhaps the dominant force in the resistance ranged against Franco's fascists. This in turn reflected the popular base of anarchism particularly in the towns and villages of Andalucia whose distance from Madrid offered a degree of autonomy and self-determination of the kind that collectivist variants of anarchism relish.

As for the contemporary political scene, anarchists are a vocal and highly visible part of the anti-capitalist movement. The 'Black Bloc', a loose coalition of militant anarchistic affinity groups, has been more or less ever-present at the larger demonstrations. Huge numbers of smaller groupings regularly participate in anti-capitalist protests as the ubiquity of anarchist papers such as *Class War*, *Total Liberty*, *Anarchy: the Journal of Desire Armed*, *Freedom*, *Here and Now*, *Organise!* (to name a small fraction) testify. There are also many anarchist umbrella groupings operating internet-based networks such as the 'Anti-Capitalist Convergence' based in North America, 'Infoshop.Org' and the 'Struggle' collective in Ireland, which serves as a focus for local protests and campaigns, including, in the case of the latter, a Zapatista solidarity campaign and newsgroup.

Such a profusion of media is itself witness to the central fact about anarchism, which is that 'anarchism' is essentially an umbrella term sheltering a staggeringly diverse range of political currents and groups. Yet the diversity of anarchism as a tradition and as a politics is rather different in nature to the diversity of the Marxist scene. Here it is less to do with *doctrinal* differences, and more to do with the very different reasons why it is possible to be opposed to the state in particular and centralised power or bureaucracy more generally. Anarchists do in fact argue over which anarchist texts are the 'key' ones; but one rarely hears or sees anarchist groups refer to themselves as say 'Bakuninite' or 'Tolstoyan' in the way Marxist groups term themselves 'Leninist', 'Maoist' or 'Trotskyist'. Indeed, to call oneself an 'anarchist' is to say very little of interest about oneself at all. One immediately needs to say what *kind* of anarchist, and in particular whether one is a collectivist or communist anarchist or an individualist or libertarian anarchist. Even with these distinctions we need to probe further, for the 'libertarian anarchist' could on the face of it *either* be in favour of capitalism or against it. Those who follow the lead of classical American anarchist thinkers of the nineteenth century, such as Benjamin Tucker, Lysander Spooner or Josiah Warren, would probably find themselves sympathising with those *inside* the conference centre at the meetings of the WTO or World Bank defending capitalism against the attacks of the anti-capitalists outside. Indeed some of the more prominent American (libertarian) anarchists would no doubt argue that there is *too much* intervention in the world rather than not enough. For a glimpse of this 'other' anarchism, just type in the names 'Ayn Rand', 'David Friedman' or 'Murray Rothbard' in *Google* and see what jumps out. *Pro*-capitalist anarchism is, as one might expect, particularly prevalent in the US where it feeds on the strong individualist and libertarian currents that have always been a part of the American political imaginary. To return to the point, however, there are individualist anarchists who are most certainly not anti-capitalist and there are those who may well be. Followers of Max Stirner, the nineteenth-century 'nihilistic egoist', would be among them, notwithstanding Marx's withering assault on his credentials to be considered a radical thinker. But we get to much more solid ground in considering the dominant tendency within anarchism, which is that of the collectivists or anarcho-communists. Of what does their anti-capitalism consist?

Anarchists regard *the continuing existence of the state as an obstacle to the development of cooperative or communal existence.* Like Marxists, they generally agree that the state is an instrument of class rule, designed and maintained to secure private property rights or, what amounts to the same, the private ownership of the means of production, the land, mines and factories. In this sense the critique of the state is often bound up with a critique of private property and of capitalism more generally. Bakunin, Proudhon and Peter Kropotkin, the three best known anarchists of the middle to late nineteenth century, were all anti-statists and anti-capitalists. Thereafter, however, anarchists tend to diverge strongly on what a 'post-capitalist' society would be like, and in particular on what principle of social organisation would be appropriate to replace the capitalist market. Kropotkin, for example was a keen advocate of 'mutualism', or the idea that cooperation is more or less innate in human nature. He envisaged forms of society that were essentially reciprocal with people working together for the common good as opposed to working for profit or the market. This is the kind of anarchism favoured by, among others, Noam Chomsky who points to the cooperative basis of social life and thus the possibility of a non-antagonistic or 'mutualist' global order. Proudhon, who developed a number of 'models', combined mutualist approaches with varieties of more or less strict egalitarianism. In his most famous work, *What is Property?* (answer: 'theft!') he argued that, since everyone is in a sense the product of society, everyone should receive equal shares from the social pot. On this logic poets would get the same as brain surgeons, as both are in some sense 'necessary' in any society as well as being the product of it.

Others have argued for limited, i.e. non capitalist markets, or for 'gift' economies in which people are encouraged to exchange without thought to 'equivalence'. One of the more popular variants of recent times follows Tolstoy and Gandhi in arguing for a return to the subsistence economy, to the idea that we should grow only as much as we need to consume. This would be particularly so for the multiple 'green' anarchisms that have sprung up since the 1970s. More generally, what tends to characterise collectivist anarchist approaches to 'post-capitalism' is a perhaps healthy dose of optimism about human motivation, and also an undogmatic or non-doctrinal approach to issues of social organisation. Few anarchists are in favour of large scale social organisation, preferring instead a variety of local or regional solutions to decision-making, together with some form of loose federative structure to tackle issues of inter-communal interest such as transportation, pollution or infrastructure needs. A constant in all anarchist approaches is, nonetheless, that any such matters can be dealt with without the need for the state, for armed intervention or the threat of it. We can and do co-operate with each other; the problem is that capitalism prevents us from doing so more extensively than at present.

'means' and 'ends'

Some or all such approaches can be regarded as more or less in keeping with those of many varieties of Marxism, particularly the more 'autonomist' kinds. It is for this reason that anarchists were able to sit alongside Marxists in the First International. Where anarchists have tended to depart from Marxists, sometimes radically so, is on the question of the 'means', of how one opposes the current system and advances to the new. The example of Bakunin is perhaps instructive in this respect. Marx's great rival in the First International, Bakunin had little difficulty recognising in Marx's thoughts on communism something akin to his own anarchism, which by contrast to Marx's was always more suggestive than firmly mapped out. Yet he consistently berated Marx on questions of organisation and strategy, and it is here that we find an echo of contemporary disputes between anarchists and Marxists. Bakunin's critique in 'Marxism, Freedom and the State' turned on three issues:

- the assumption that it is the experience of alienation or exploitation at the hands of the capitalist class that generated the desire to overcome capitalism;
- the identification of the working class as the agent of change to the exclusion of all others;
- the necessity for a state to guide the transition from capitalism to communism.

Bakunin opposed all three, setting a template for the more militant forms of anarchism we find in the contemporary anti-capitalist movement. He argued that:

- the desire to overcome oppression is a *universal* feature of human existence and thus to be found at least potentially in all individuals irrespective of class background or designation. Bakunin anticipated later neo-Marxists such as Marcuse, Negri, Deleuze and Guattari in pointing to the revolutionary potential of the 'riff-raff' or 'multitude' and thus opposed the privileged position accorded the working class in the Marxist revolutionary schema.
- the working class is as a *class* often amongst the *least* revolutionary elements of society, being content to agitate for better working conditions, health and safety regulations and enhanced pensions.
- the state cannot be deployed for revolutionary ends. Power has a tendency to corrupt even the most 'virtuous' of revolutionaries.

The vitriol was not all directed one way. As Marx persistently argued, Bakunin's libertarian rhetoric was sharply at odds with his own recommendations for revolution which variously turned on the use of conspiratorial groups, assassinations, subterranean plots, subterfuge and revolutionary violence. Indeed Bakunin's reputation was permanently damaged by his association with the Russian terrorist

Nechaev, the author of the notorious 'Catechism of a Revolutionary', which argued for indiscriminate use of terror to destabilise the existing state of affairs.

Such disputes and contradictions survive in contemporary relations between anarchists and Marxists, and indeed within anarchism itself. One of the most contentious issues as regards the latter is *the use of violence as an instrument of resistance*. Those advocating violence sometimes known as 'Spikies' have clashed with the 'Fluffies' or those who advocate non-violent forms of direct action to advance the anti-capitalist cause. Within the spikier element there are those who distinguish between violence to property (such as McDonald's restaurants and other 'corporate' property) and violence to persons, particularly the police and army, regarded by many militant anarchists as a legitimate target. In order to accommodate such differences of approach some anti-capitalist protests have been split into various different marches by the organisers. At Prague for example, this led to the disaggregation of protest itself. There was a 'blue' march for spikier elements, a 'yellow' march for direct action groupings such as *Ya Basta!* and a 'pink and silver' march for those such as the 'Tactical Frivolity' group who are completely 'fluffy'. There were various other actions as well, some confrontational, others more 'frivolous' still. Thus at the same 'action' the police were confronted by black-clad paramilitary groups, WOMBLES and *Tuti Bianchi* wearing 'white overalls' stuffed with protective padding and 'pink fairies' skipping about, singing and throwing glitter in the air.

The question of means and ends is hugely complex, and tends particularly in the anarchist movement to elicit the wildest possible variations, in turn emphasising the point that 'anarchism' is a loose label rather than a consistent doctrine or ideology. Reflecting these differences it has to be accepted that there is a world of difference between the views of the Stirnerite 'egoist', the Kropotkinite collectivist and the Tolstoyan Christian anarchist. This is part of the fascination as well as part of the frustration of anarchism 'in practice'. On the other hand, it would be wrong to imply that this diversity makes anarchism an ineffective or inconsequential body of ideas. As is evident, some of the most positive aspects of the contemporary anti-capitalist resistance have a largely anarchistic character. One thinks here of the *nature* and *form* of the large scale discussions of the first World Social Forum, the participants of which refused to become a 'bureaucratic' standing organisation of the kind that characterises traditional political parties and movements. Everyone has to be heard, and have her say. No one can be represented or 'spoken for' by some official, intellectual or otherwise privileged 'comrade'. Whilst this makes for necessarily 'anarchic' occasions with little in the way of permanent monuments to celebrate, at the same time it is precisely the uncompromisingly collective nature of proceedings that to many anarchists imbue them with a legitimacy and standing that it would otherwise be difficult to match. To those who completely reject the possibility and desirability of doctrinal or ideological 'truth', the apparently shambolic nature of such meetings is the necessary price to be paid for its moral or ethical credibility as a counter-force to every kind of bureaucratic organisation whether capitalist or anti-capitalist in orientation. Living free from 'ideology', from 'representatives' is what counts, and if this means having to put up with interminable meetings attempting to bash out some sort of consensus on the way forward, then so be it. This is what a non-capitalist world *should* be like.

Thinking more concretely, there is now huge interest within anti-capitalist circles in the development of alternative economic systems springing up around both the developed and 'developing' world, many of which have their origins in anarchist thought and activity. We could mention here the idea of alternative or 'parallel' trading schemes that undercut or dispense with capitalistic forms of commerce, and also the efforts of many economists such as those associated with the 'participatory economics' or 'ParEcon' initiative to develop trading schemes with a decidedly anarchistic air to them. Examples of the former include the use of labour notes whose units of denomination translate into labour hours. Within host areas, people are able to exchange products, goods and services without recourse to official currency and thus without recourse to banks, interest rates and the apparatus of 'capitalist exploitation'. There are Local Exchange and Trading Schemes' (LETS), barter schemes, and informal gift economies where people sign up to offer services or goods on a more or less benevolent basis. Such non-profit based forms of exchange are often very close to the kind of economic arrangements suggested by anarchists such as Proudhon and Kropotkin. Both argued that such schemes were a key to undermining capitalism and to establishing economic relations based on a different value system, one based on mutuality, trust and 'real' equality. Such schemes are experiments in another way of living and organising social life. Their growing popularity across both developed and developing worlds demonstrates the continuing relevance of 'anarchistic' proposals and practices notwithstanding the lack of agreement amongst anarchists themselves as to how to produce 'anarchism'.

deep, deeper, deepest 'green'

As we noted in the last chapter, one of the most important currents to have emerged out of the post-68 realignment of politics is that of environmentalism or ecologism. The 'ism' appendage here should however not be taken to imply that there is some straightforward position to be unearthed or unpacked. Far from it. 'Green' politics is a complex and sometimes conflicting amalgam of ideas that produces equally vociferous debates amongst its advocates. It is also worth bearing in mind that greens need not necessarily be anti-capitalist, and there are a great many who are not. These are regarded as 'light' greens as opposed to the 'deep' greens who frequently *are* anti-capitalist in orientation. Amongst the most important currents to note here are various American groups, in particular Earth First!, perhaps the largest and best known of the militant deep green collectives. We need also to mention the various 'primitivist' groups who follow prominent thinkers such as John Zerzan, the author of *Future Primitive* and father figure to the *Green Anarchy* collective that also publishes the essays of other primitivists such as Eric Blair and Feral Faun. We also need to mention the 'social ecologists' influenced by the work of Murray Bookchin. There are also numerous eco-marxist, eco-feminist or eco-socialist groupings, though they lack the organisational visibility of groups like Earth First! Some of these are theoretically 'hybrid' positions in that they combine elements from Marxism, autonomism or, more frequently, anarchism.

Many of these groups and collectives have been present at anti-capitalist carnivals, as well as the Earth summits and the various environmental protests they help organise. One should also bear in mind that there are many radical or anti-capitalist greens operating primarily within the official green parties (usually as 'fundis', as opposed to the 'realos' or realists), and also within many of the more prominent NGOs such as Greenpeace and Friends of the Earth. This is to say nothing about the wholly or largely unaffiliated activists who are the mainstay of many of the direct action protests against environmental degradation across the developed and developing world. Indeed the contrast between green activism and Marxist activism is acute at this point. Many greens would see themselves primarily as 'doers', as activists working *directly* to prevent the harmful effects of capitalist production, rather than as working for an *organisation* ('the Party') that will at some further point in time 'lead' us to a post-capitalist future. From this point of view, their activism is often even more 'unofficial', non- or post-ideological and loose limbed than those mentioned above.

The contrast with Marxist anti-capitalism is, however, much more acute at the level of ideology. Earlier in the chapter we noted that one of the distinguishing features of Marxism is not merely its acceptance of industrialisation and modernisation as requirements of socialism and thence communism, but its belief that without them the latter are impossible pipe-dreams. Indeed Marx reserved some of his harshest criticism for 'romantic' anti-capitalists and 'utopian socialists' who imagined that a better society could be constructed before capitalism had run its course. Communism for Marx is a hyper-industrial society, a society that is able to satisfy needs however expressed whilst lowering the amount of time needed to produce necessary goods. This could only be achieved on the back of capitalism's relentless industrialising and modernising drive that in turn improved dramatically the productive potential available to humanity. It is partly for this reason that once it became apparent the much awaited global revolution had been 'postponed', the Bolshevik regime wasted little time in expending its energies and the energies of the Russian people on an effort to industrialise as rapidly as possible (Lenin: 'Communism equals Soviet power plus *electrification*'). Industry was the key to socialism and the better life to come. From this point of view the emergence of the deep greens in the wake of 1968 was as a reaction to the 'super-industrialism' shared by advocates of both capitalism and communism. As we noted in the last chapter, the 1973 Oil Crisis encouraged a rethinking of 'sustainability' and the limits to growth. At its most radical this rethinking prompted two currents of relevance for our purposes, one eco-centric and the other anthropo-centric.

Eco-centric thought, often strongly influenced by the work of James Lovelock who developed the 'Gaia' hypothesis stresses the necessity for regarding the Earth as 'prior' to the humans who inhabit it. This notion of priority is not just temporal or chronological in the sense that the existence of the Earth is literally prior to the arrival of human species, but philosophically and existentially prior as well. The Earth is in this sense 'first'. We need to abandon thinking of the earth as a resource for us, as a 'common storehouse' (as described in, for example, the Bible), or a gigantic warehouse that we can just use up at will. The Earth has rather to be thought of as a complex totality, of which we are merely a part, though a part with the potential to destroy as well as preserve life. From this point of view the objection to capitalism should already be clear. Capitalism perpetuates indeed celebrates the storehouse idea, seeing the world as a resource for exploitation for the purpose of private gain.

As a description of how capitalism works in practice, there is little to argue with in this image. As we noted in the first chapter, the effect of competition, particularly intense competition, is to drive out considerations of the *implicit* worth or value of resources such as rainforests or rare species. To the capitalist, such resources have a value insofar as they can be exploited and sold in the market place. Rainforests have a value primarily as timber, which in turn can be sold for a profit in the global market-place for wood products. To eco-centric activists, capitalism has to be combated in order to reverse the ethical priority of the market over the earth. Whatever damages or threatens the earth must be challenged, which in the case of Earth First! means direct action against loggers or timber workers, if necessary by 'monkey-wrenching' – the dismantling of machinery. It also implies the deployment of a moral calculus of a particularly controversial kind, for what is also implicit in the eco-centric pos-ition is a more or less egalitarian stance as between species. It is *Earth* first, not humanity-first, which in turn implies that what is natural is good. Thus, should 'nature' offer solutions to population growth such as AIDS or monsoons or plagues, then nature should be allowed to take its 'course'. Indeed why should the mosquito carrying the plague be regarded as of 'lesser' value at all, if it is accepted that all species have the same value? This is an extreme working out of a certain kind of eco-centric logic found in such groups; but it shows, firstly, the undeniably radical nature of what is on offer, and, sec-ondly, the degree to which the world would have to change or be remade in order to give life to the ideology. Necessary measures would include:

• cessation of the exploitation of natural resources in favour of a harmonious relationship between humanity and the planet;

- end of production for profit in favour of de-industrialised solutions that prioritise the preservation of the 'wilderness';
- end of state-centric solutions to questions of organisation, infrastructure, collective provision of all kinds. Social organisation to be non-hierarchical, non-dominating, decentralised.

Anthropo-centric approaches that are more 'humanistic' in orientation can be just as radical as eco-centric ones. 'Primitivism', which has risen in prominence amongst environmental anti-capitalists in recent years argues for a complete rejection of industry and technology and thus for a return back to the 'simplest' possible forms of life. Here again the object of the critique is the 'industrialism' of both capitalism and communism, both of which assert the necessity for 'progress' and the utilisation of technology for 'human' benefit. Such 'benefits' are explicitly queried by Zerzan who follows a line of counter-Enlightenment theorists such as Tolstoy and Marcuse in seeing us as enslaved to the technological 'machine'. In his view, if we are serious about constructing a post-capitalism built on genuine equality, the obliteration of hierarchy and bureaucracy in the name of a richness of existence, then we need to recognise the pernicious and debilitating effect of industry – indeed 'civilization' – itself ('For the Destruction of Civilization – For Reconnection to Life!'). In this sense Zerzan is unafraid of the charge that supporters of capitalism have often made against anti-capitalist radicals, which is that in opposing 'economic growth' or 'development' they would necessarily forfeit the advantages that come from competition in terms of the trickle down of technological benefits such as new medicines, or faster computers. For him the 'advantages' are hollow and illusory compared to a life restored to the 'wild'.

Moving away from the radical end of the spectrum, there are many more moderate though still 'anti-capitalist' variations on both the eco-centric and anthropo-centric positions that have their supporters. Indeed it would be an exaggeration to imply that ultra-radical positions such as those of Earth First! and the primitivists are necessarily dominant amongst environmentalists despite their high profile. Looking at eco-activist materials what becomes apparent is that there is a tendency to avoid grandiose ideological positions altogether in favour of a pragmatic, and non-ideological stance in relation to the question of 'post-capitalist' alternatives. A defence of the concept of 'sustainability' as against the excesses of capitalism in its relentless quest to transform the planet into exchange values is evidently enough to 'sustain' a variety of radical currents and activisms. Indeed, as is also apparent environmentalists often hitch their wagon to traditions of thought such as Marxism, anarchism and feminism in an effort to refine both the nature of the critique of capitalism offered and the kind of world that they wish to see 'liberated' or created. Yet, what seems clear is that radical environmental activism is primarily *practical* and *immediate* for many of its most enthusiastic followers. There are many ways in which environmentalists can achieve a sense of worth and satisfaction in the here and now, for example through blocking building programmes, lobbying on behalf of an endangered species, saving a forest or a green space, hosting street carnivals to 'reclaim the streets' or mass bike rides to underscore the necessity for sustainable transport. In this sense even radical environmentalists can at times sound curiously *apolitical*, as if *all* that mattered was saving 'the turtles' or the rainforests. To those who care deeply about such issues, this may *indeed* be all that matters, in the same way that a mother without food for her children may well be completely unconcerned about where the food has come from or how it was manufactured.

What the above indicates is that there is something very particular about green radicalism as opposed to say Marxist or anarchist activism. This is that it is predominantly *non-* or *post-ideological.* Many greens are happy enough to say that if you want an argument against capitalism, then just look at the state of the world, look at what capitalists *do.* As we noted in the last chapter, it is this resolutely non-ideological aspect of environmental activism that is one of its great attractions for those wearied by what seems like the internal wrangling and self-serving of other kinds of radicalism. But what it means is that radical environmentalism tends to concentrate more on what is wrong with the present than on how the present is to be changed for the better. Or else, it seems dimly suggestive of something else such as anarchism or socialism, in which case it might with some legitimacy be asked what exactly is 'green' about green anti-capitalism? On the other hand if this implies that there is a strong commonality between say anarchists and radical greens – as perhaps embodied in the work of Kropotkin, E.F. Schumacher or William Morris – then this has the considerable merit of keeping lines of communication and alliance open, in turn permitting the forms of broad-based, '(dis)organised' action that groups such as Reclaim the Streets and Critical Mass have promoted with considerable impact over the past decade or so.

On the face of it a chapter on contemporary revolutionary positions that covers red, black and green anti-capitalisms might be thought to more or less exhaust the subject. It does not. One of the most obvious omissions is that of feminism. Many feminists will no doubt look at the male author of the book and say 'typical'. In defence, many feminists themselves note the difficulty of identifying a distinctly feminist 'post-capitalism', as opposed to the numerous varieties of Marxist feminism, anarcho-feminism and eco-feminism acting and interacting within each sub-radicalism. This is not to say that women play anything like a lesser role in the anti-capitalist protests. Far from it. It is clear that women are every bit as engaged in anti-capitalist resistances as are men, in some cases more so. It is to say that radical anti-capitalist feminism has tended to annex itself – or become annexed to – sub-radicalisms. There are numerous reasons why this might be the case. One suggestion is that with the fragmentation of the feminist movement itself in the late 1970s and 1980s, many radical feminists moved down the 'single-issue' road, embarking on campaigns against various legal, political, economic or social inequalities. Another is that feminists sought common cause with others to advance the interests of women beneath red, black or green 'umbrellas'. Whatever the case, it will be interesting to see whether a radical anti-capitalist feminism does develop to take its place alongside the sub-groupings we have in fact covered.

ya basta!: a brief excursus on marcos and 'zapatismo'

A different 'problem' is created by the case of the Zapatistas, who we have not so far covered in our brief review of radical anti-capitalisms. As is probably obvious, there is a strong temptation for political theorists like myself to subordinate what emerges today to ideas that existed in the past, sometimes the far-flung past. Contemporary anarchists (say) sound a lot like anarchists of the past and so one is tempted to assume they must in some strong sense *be* the same, when they might not be. The same is true for Marxism which has a similarly strong link to the past; rather less so environmentalism, which is much more a product of the contemporary world, notwithstanding those 'echoes' of the past. With the

Zapatistas, however, even know-it-all theorists have to recognise that something tangibly novel is afoot, even if (yes) one can hear the occasional echo. They are clearly not Marxists, not anarchists and not environmentalists. Nor is their stance some muddy mixture of all three, or some sublime *Über*-radicalism that somehow takes the 'best' or most significant elements and transcends them all. There is something starkly *new* about Zapatismo that demands that it be treated for what it is. We should also note that the Zapatistas occupy a place in the affections of anti-capitalists that other groups and positions do not. Marxists argue with anarchists who argue with environmentalists, who argue with reformists, and so forth. Indeed, despite the common cause, enmities, some of them ancient, still flicker beneath the surface of exchanges between 'camps', reminding us of the difficulty involved in reconciling different philosophies and world views to the same political cause. But when it comes to the Zapatistas, it is noticeable that at the very least there is considerable respect not only for what they have done, but more intriguingly what they 'represent'. It is time to unveil the mysteries for the impatient beginner, who may by now be thoroughly irritated by the whole subject. Who are the Zapatistas and what makes them so unique?

To begin with some context, the Zapatistas are the latter day inheritors of the mantle of Emiliano Zapata, one of the leaders of the Mexican revolution of 1910. Zapata's programme was a simple yet radical one. He wanted to challenge the ownership of land which then as now was monopolised by a small number of families, who had inherited their vast riches from the Spanish *Conquistadores*. Zapata was ultimately unsuccessful and indeed he was later murdered by conservative forces led by Colonel Guajardo. The dream of land redistribution nevertheless lived on and was later taken up by an insurgent guerrilla force, the Ejército Zapatista de Liberación Nacional (EZLN) or Zapatistas. A seemingly ramshackle melange of students, intellectuals, radicals and indigenous peasant rebels, the Zapatistas emerged from the jungle of the Chiapas region in 1994 within hours of the signing of the NAFTA agreement, hounding the Mexican federal forces from the region. Since 1994 there has been something of a stand-off between the EZLN and the Mexican state, which in the glare of the world's media seems unable and unwilling to attempt to root out the Zapatistas from the difficult mountainous terrain of the Chiapas. The result has been that the latter have not merely maintained an insurgent presence in the region, but created a zone based on principles thrashed out between the indigenous peoples and senior Zapatista leaders such as Subcomandante Insurgente Marcos. This is to say that within Mexico, a relatively industrialised country of one-hundred million people, the Zapatistas have established what is effectively an autonomous area governed by an entirely different set of principles and norms, indeed a different philosophy, to the rest of the country. It is difficult to think of parallels in what is now supposed to be a 'global village' dominated by corporate interests. It is difficult to think too of a parallel for Marcos who since 1994 has orchestrated communications between the Zapatistas and the outside world. It is Marcos who has translated an otherwise homespun and admittedly pragmatic set of principles into what is now termed 'Zapatismo', something that is part poetry, part philosophy, part rebel folklore. What then is Zapatismo, and what is its significance for the matters under review?

As Marcos describes the situation himself, he left Mexico city as an impatient and idealistic student full of Marxian and quasi-Marxian ideas about how to liberate the indigenous peoples and embark on a revolution that would sweep away Mexico's creaking political establishment. Yet having made it to the mountains and jungles of the Chiapas and telling the people he met what it was that was required for their 'emancipation', he found himself listening to what it was that they were telling him. He quickly realised that they effectively 'knew' everything they needed to know about how they should live, how they wanted to live, and thus that they had no need for his advice let alone his 'leadership'. What they lacked was the *means* by which they could live their lives according to their own needs, interests and traditions. From this simple reversal of roles, Marcos seems to have evolved an entire 'non-philosophy' based on 'listening' rather than 'speaking for'. This already sounds rather obscure so, for the sake of getting clear about what is novel here, let's go back and recall some of what we have just been covering above.

Recall the theme of the chapter. We are discussing radical ideas about emancipation, liberation, freedom. In particular we have been contrasting ideologies. We said at the outset that possessing an ideology is like possessing an image or painting of how the world should look. Those who possess an ideology want the rest of us to see that the painting is in some important sense 'true', that it accurately pictures a world most if not all of us would recognise as desirable if not 'ideal'. We might for some reason not see it that way yet; but we will, or we will once we begin to see things 'clearly'. This puts the possessor of an ideology in a privileged position – but also an invidious one – vis-à-vis those who are yet to be convinced. He or she needs them to see the truth of the picture in order to bring the picture about; he or she needs to convince them of the truth or desirability of the underlying analysis and account of how the world could be better. Failing this, then the canvas remains just that, a picture or image, and not a *reality*. In order to change the world people need to be *mobilised* behind a set of ideas. Failing that the world will remain the same.

To return to Marcos's tale, it became obvious to him that what the indigenous people wanted was not a new ideology, but release *from* an ideology, namely neoliberalism. The Zapatista revolt was in this sense a revolt *against* neoliberalism in the form of the NAFTA agreement which would make the life of Mexico's poor even more miserable than it already was. Yet more than this, he began to see that the issue was not just about neoliberal ideology, but ideology more generally, and in particular revolutionary ideology. What struck him was that the peoples of the Chiapas *already knew* how they would like to live. They simply wanted to run their own affairs rather than being pushed around by outsiders. This did not just mean the big landowners, the Mexican federal government, or the big corporations who would now be unleashed on the basis of the NAFTA agreement. 'Outsiders' also and of necessity meant revolutionaries, indeed those with the very 'best interests' of the peasants at heart. Those like Marcos who were sensitive to what it was that the peasants actually wanted, as opposed to what it was that they *should* want, saw that their job was to do nothing more than ensure that what the peasants themselves wanted to see happen, happened. In short, he very consciously gave up the position of the revolutionary, the ideologist, the intellectual with a pre-packaged solution or idea of how the peasants should live. One of his communiqués in 2002 was entitled 'I shit on all the Revolutionary Vanguards', underpinning the extent to which Marcos had not merely broken from the 'revolutionary tradition' but begun to see it as an obstacle to the development of resistance. The Zapatistas thus enacted a *post*-ideological form of politics centred on guaranteeing a space within which the indigenous peoples could organise their own affairs and indeed organise the affairs of the Zapatistas whose own rationale was now nothing more – though certainly nothing less – than ensuring the integrity of the autonomous zone itself.

What are the ramifications of such a stance in terms of what we are considering here?

zapatismo and 'post-ideology'

As a post-ideological politics Zapatismo effectively renounces the superstructure of expectations that have informed political philosophy since Plato invented the Philosopher Kings. This is to say that it has forsaken the idea that knowledge or understanding can give a superior insight into issues concerning how we should live and, thus, that, for example, I as a political theorist with twenty or so years' worth of heavy reading behind me, have the right or the role to 'legislate' on behalf of others. It means that what the intellectuals or the 'vanguards' say is simply one set of views to be considered (or not) alongside everyone else's views – no matter how ridiculous, incomprehensible, outlandish or outrageous the latter may seem. Everyone's voice has in this sense equal weight and an equal right to be heard. If this sounds quite a lot like a certain kind of democratic liberalism, then in a sense it is. But Marcos insistently poses the questions: which liberal is it that actually wants the unmediated voice to be decisive? Which liberal thinks that voices are more important than structures, institutions and constitutions? Which liberal is it that wants the 'voice' to be heard on every matter facing the community, whether it be the kind of crops to be sown or the direction of military strategy? Which liberal is *really* prepared to hear everyone's voice, without the 'convenience' of representatives to give sense or 'wisdom' to them? Certainly not the neoliberals. The problem is that liberalism *in practice* is quite a different proposition to democratic liberalism *in theory*, which in turn explains the success of liberalism in establishing itself as the dominant or hegemonic idea of the modern world. They *say* they are listening, but are they *really*?

As it pans out in practice, Zapatismo looks a lot less like 'liberalism' and a lot more like certain versions of anarchism, autonomism and environmentalism. Within the zone, for example, the forty communes or villages 'exercise power' as Marcos puts it, meaning that the villages run their own affairs on the basis of discussions held at village or commune level. Inter-communal or zonal affairs are handled by what are termed Clandestine Revolutionary Indigenous Committees (CCRIs) elected on direct democratic principles. But even the meetings of the CCRIs are open to any and all *compañeros* who wish to make themselves heard. Decision-making appears to follow the principle, if not of unanimity then of overwhelming consensus, with dissenting voices entertained until such time as general agreement is reached. This makes for long, indeed sometimes interminable, meetings; but the feeling seems to be that this is the necessary price for reaching outcomes which are satisfactory to the communities themselves. It should be added that the Zapatistas are themselves answerable to the CCRIs, with military strategy worked out by a similar process of deliberation. Yet what is noticeable is that despite the clearly anarchistic basis of decision-making, anarchists have been amongst those most ambivalent in their reaction to the Zapatistas. Why could this possibly be? Isn't this anarchy 'in action' and thus a cause for celebration? It is here that we begin to see how Zapatismo is different as an approach to revolutionary politics to what has gone before.

The dilemma for anarchists, Marxists and others committed to a given vision of how the world should look should be apparent. This is that, to recall, Marcos and the Zapatistas are not *actually* committed to a particular vision of the world. As they made startlingly clear in one of their earliest pronouncements, they are committed 'to the creation of a world in which *all* worlds are possible'. This means they are not committed to anarchy, to direct democracy, to the socialisation of production as such. Nor are they committed to peasant farming or the CCRIs in principle. They are committed to getting rid of the grip of one particular ideology, neoliberalism, so that other visions are made possible. They are committed to giving everyone a voice, and a stake in the world. In this sense they are committed to something much less elaborate than an ideology but, as they put it, to the simple values of 'dignity' and 'respect', and this in turn means *not presuming to know in advance* what it is that the voice wants or needs. It presumes that one is going to *listen* to the voices, not ignore them. As we noted above, Zapatismo is in this sense a non-philosophy or non-doctrine. It has no recommendations to make, no final answers to the great problems of life. Zapatismo concerns the creation of *autonomous space* rather than *ideas about autonomy*. It seeks to create spaces or to enlarge those that already exist within which people can exercise their own autonomy. In this sense it finds itself in direct opposition to another 'spatial' political project, namely neoliberalism. Neoliberals argue in favour of an enlargement of the *sphere* of free trade, bringing the 'benefits' of the market to the globe. Neoliberalism appears as a morally and ethically neutral project. Its spokespeople say it is 'beyond ideology', that it is only concerned with allowing people access to the market and thus to the means by which their own dreams and needs can be fulfilled. Economic globalisation, we are told, is about drawing the world together, creating 'a new space'; but not telling them what to do with it. What seems evident is that the potential power of Zapatismo lies in this ability to match the 'discursive power' of neoliberalism and free market ideology. The rhetoric of space it employs is a rhetoric in which the freedom to decide remains intact, the freedom to choose, the freedom to be heard. The difference is, as seems clear from the experience of the Chiapas, that it is not *just* rhetoric; they mean it.

If all this seems impossibly utopian and other-worldly, then it is. This is one of its charms, and why so many have invested so many hopes and fears in the continued ability of the Zapatistas to hold the Mexican federal forces at bay. What such investments paper over is the problem of advancing a 'post-ideological' project of the kind represented by Zapatismo. It is only fair to enumerate what such problems might amount to so that we get a sense of why it is that more ideologically committed groups have a problem with it. Such groups argue that:

- A post-ideological stance is politically *disabling*. It means that activists are required to give up offering a positive alternative account of how the world might look in favour of a *negative* or oppositional stance against something else (i.e. neoliberalism). This is to say that the force of the message is *reactive*, not active as many radicals think it should be.
- Activists are prey to the immediate, perhaps uncritical wishes of its constituency. One of the tensions in the Zapatista zone has, for example, been the place of women in decision-making and, indeed, in social life more generally. Many women have been an active presence in the struggle, yet many men wish their wives and partners would stay at home playing the part of the traditional mother. This in turn creates a tension between the EZLN which itself has embraced the role of women in the struggle and some of the men who are unwilling to let go of their 'traditional' views. Lacking a doctrine or clear ideology inevitably leaves the Zapatistas open to the charge that they are arbitrarily siding with one part of the community against another, without the mandate of either.

- Renouncing a 'leadership' function for themselves makes the 'Zapatismo' itself look like a localised solution for a local problem, and thus in turn one living on borrowed time. As they put it themselves, they are not interested in 'capturing power', only ensuring that the people of the Chiapas are able to 'exercise' it. Is this then to say that they are not interested in extending the struggle to the rest of the region or to the rest of Mexico – or the rest of the world? If so, why should the political elites in Mexico City be worried? No leadership function means no threat of the Zapatistas breaking out of their zone to nurture, support and help neighbouring insurgents. 'Let them *have* the Chiapas.'

Such criticisms are rarely offered with the purpose of belittling the Zapatista 'achievement', though of course Marcos is surely entitled to respond in appropriately robust fashion ('I shit on all the Revolutionary Vanguards' ...). What such queries perhaps highlight is that the advancement of a non- or post-ideological position is not without its own difficulties, as if merely renouncing 'ideology' as such would somehow make it easier to develop a post-capitalist alternative. As is clear, it won't. Or at least it won't in all cases and in all places, as some are tempted to think. What the Zapatista case tells us, however, is that a post- or non-ideological position *can* be enough for a significant and effective mobilisation, particularly where the 'enemy' is clearly defined and perceived in such terms. Here lie some clues to the Zapatista's success in their own 'zone':

- They are reacting to widely, almost universally perceived injust-ices, in this case the retention of land and resources by non-indigenous families and corporate interests;
- They are seeking to defend or restore a way of life against centuries of abuse and maltreatment at the hands of 'settlers';
- They seek to reenact practices of decision-making that were widely presumed to work.

In short, they are defending an indigenously held 'ideology' or cultural practice against those of the Mexican political and economic elites, albeit with some modifications to ensure that 'new' concerns are respected or taken on board, such as the position of women. It will be interesting to reflect the degree to which such conditions are operative elsewhere.

conclusion

This has been a long discussion and we need to think about what, if anything, has been learned. I mentioned at the start of chapter three that there is general acceptance that there is no anti-capitalist movement as such, only at best a 'movement of movements'. I also suggested that underneath the umbrella lay diverse, plural and conflicting accounts of how the anti-capitalist resistance should proceed. What should be obvious having overviewed a sample of some of the currents on offer is the sheer degree of plurality and thus the ever-present scope for conflict between the different radical currents. Indeed it is probably true to say that the only matter they all agree on is that capitalism should be opposed. *How* it should be opposed, by what means and to what ends is the subject of profound and sometimes bitter dissensus. What is also clear, however, is that as radical currents 'de-ideologise' or move from the top of the vertical plane to the bottom, it is possible to identify certain themes and currents in common. Looking over the accounts of libertarian Marxism, autonomism, anarchism, certain kinds of green radicalism and towards Zapatismo, there are definite points of contact and coalescence. These might be summarised as follows:

- Economic affairs need to be *re-politicised*: made subject to the needs, wants and desires of both consumers *and* producers.
- People need to be *re-empowered*: given the opportunity to take part in vital decisions regarding their own affairs.
- Power needs to be *re-localised*: power should be closer to the people, not abstracted away to national governments or global structures unaccountable to those below.
- Decisions need to be *re-popularised*: elite rule should give way to forms of interaction that permit the circulation or flow of decision-making capacity amongst ordinary people themselves.

Quite a lot of this concerns the *form* that power or decision-making should take, rather than the substance or the outcomes. If there is a common theme to both radical and reformist anti-capitalism then it is the *primacy of the political* over the purely economic and thus the need to recuperate power from those who have annexed it through support for a depoliticised 'free market'. We need more 'politics', not less. We need more discussion, more occasions to participate than is currently granted by the 'new rulers of the world'. But how is politics to be reborn? How can such an intuitively felt observation, shared by so many, become the basis for a global movement that is *effective* as well as, well, noisy?

resources

read on

Michael Albert, *ParEcon: Life After Capitalism* (London and New York: Verso, 2003).

Anon., 'Chiapas Revealed', www.struggle.ws/mexico/pdf/revealed1.html

Mikhail Bakunin, *Marxism, Freedom and the State* (1867), various editions, available online at: www.dwardmac.pitzer.edu/anarchist_archives/bakunin/marxnfree.html

Hakim Bey, *T.A.Z.: The Temporary Autonomous Zone, Ontological Anarchy, Poetic Terrorism* (New York: Semiotext(e), 1991).

Murray Bookchin, *The Murray Bookchin Reader* (New York: Continuum Books, 1997).

Daniel Bensaid, *A Marx for our Times: Adventures and Misadventures of a Critique* (London and New York: Verso, 2002).

Alex Callinicos, *The Revolutionary Ideas of Karl Marx* (London: Bookmarks, 1995).

Harry Cleaver, *Reading Capital Politically* (San Francisco: AK Press, 2000 [1979]).

Andrew Dobson, *Green Political Thought* (London: Routledge, 1995).

Jack Grassby, *Revolution in the 21st Century* (Washington, UK: TUPS Books, 2003).

Gill Hands, *Marx: A Beginner's Guide* (London: Headway, 2000).

Michael Hardt and Antonio Negri, *Empire* (Harvard: HUP, 2000).

John Holloway and Eloine Pelaez (eds), *Zapatista: Reinventing Revolution in Mexico* (London: Pluto Press, 1998).

Leszek Kolakowski, *Main Currents of Marxism*, 3 vols (Oxford: Oxford Paperbacks, 1981).

V.I. Lenin, *Essential Works of Lenin: What is to be Done? and Other Writings* (London: Dover, 1987).

Subcomandante Insurgente Marcos, *Our Word is Our Weapon: Selected Writings* (London: Serpent's Tail, 2002).

Peter Marshall, *Demanding the Impossible: A History of Anarchism* (London: Fontana Press, 1993).

William Morris, *News from Nowhere* (1890), various editions. Full text available online at: www.marxists.org/archive/morris/works/1890/nowhere/nowhere.htm

E.F. Schumacher, *Small is Beautiful: Economics as if People Mattered* (London: Vintage, 1993 [1973]).

Sean Sheehan, *Anarchism* (London: Reaktion Books, 2003).

Steve Wright, *Storming Heaven: Class Composition and Struggle in Italian Autonomist Marxism* (London: Pluto Press, 2002).

John Zerzan, *Future Primitive and Other Essays* (New York: Semiotext(e), 1994).

link to

www.marxists.org

www.marxism.org

www.swp.org.uk (Socialist Workers Party, UK)

www.lists.village.virginia.edu/~spoons/marxism/marxism.html (Marxist resources)

www.wombles.org.uk

www.yabasta.it

www.lists.village.virginia.edu/~spoons/aut_html/aut_02.html (autonomist resources)

www.struggle.ws (anarchist resources)

www.dwardmac.pitzer.edu/Anarchist_Archives/(classic anarchist texts)

www.parecon.org

www.earthfirst.org

www.greenanarchy.org

www.eco-action.org

www.ezln.org

www.chiapas.mediosindependientes.org (Indymedia, Chiapas)

www.reclaimthestreets.net

the future(s) of anti-capitalism

problems and perspectives

We noted in the opening section of chapter three that there is some difficulty in describing the anti-capitalist 'movement' as a movement at all. The 'it' in question is a 'movement of movements', a shifting, mobile 'assemblage' of different currents of thought, different groups and organisations, some allied to the interests of a nation-state or regional agenda, others genuinely 'global' in scope and orientation. There are groups with clear ideologically driven goals, and others with specific injustices they wish to remedy or confront, but little idea of how the world should 'look'. Some are clearly anti-capitalist, others are anti-neoliberal or anti-corporate. Others are anti-something much more local or specific than 'capitalism', neoliberal or otherwise. There are groups that focus on lobbying governments and international organisations, others that pursue their goals through direct action. Indeed there are some for whom 'direct action' is a way of life and end in itself. There are red, green and black groups, and some that somehow manage to combine all three. Just listing these various differences is to be reminded of the essentially kaleidoscopic nature of anti-capitalism, the fact that it defies easy labelling, framing or description. Even with these difficulties in mind, a 'beginner' will still, quite understandably, want to know where it is all heading or, more realistically, where it *could* be heading.

In this final chapter we need to think about what the possibilities are for the contemporary anti-capitalist movement given what we have already remarked upon in terms of its structure and organisational characteristics. But what needs to be borne in mind is that it is not just the structure and characteristics that will have a bearing on the question. This is to say that how the movement develops is not just a matter of the *internal* dynamics of the movement and the forms of collective action it is able to sustain or nourish in advancing an anti-capitalist cause. There are various '*externalities*' that also shape prospects for an anti-capitalist resistance. The most pressing of the latter would be, firstly, *the position of the USA in global politics*, and secondly, the difficulty of dealing with the *increasingly mobile nature of transnational capitalism*. We need to pause for a moment to consider these two externalities in isolation from the issues concerning *movement dynamics and the problem of collective action* that forms the bulk of the discussion in the rest of the chapter, not least because such issues will have a strong bearing on any evaluation of how the anti-capitalist movement should develop. How do these externalities impinge on the issues under discussion?

the position of the US in global politics

As we have noted on many occasions, the US is pivotal to the survival of global capitalism in its current form. Whether one likes it or not (and of course many anti-capitalists do not), the US is in military terms and in terms of any other indicator of power the most powerful state in the world. Indeed it is the most powerful state that has ever existed. The USA is, moreover, often cast as a 'lonely superpower', lonely both in the sense of being the only true superpower and also in the perception of many in the US elite that she is alone in the world: without true friends or allies to be counted upon (Britain is perhaps the only exception). Since '9/11' the US has embarked on a 'War against Terrorism'. But this is a war not only against those who are terrorists, it is as George Bush Jnr said in his statement on National Security Strategy in 2002, a war against those who may *become* terrorists. It is in his own description a 'preventive war', a war against anyone and anything that *may* be a threat to America and her interests. Such a formula changes the nature of the 'War' dramatically. A preventive war is effectively a war without end, without bounds, without a time frame. It is war that will be waged until terrorism *and* the prospect of terrorism has been 'eliminated', which, as anyone with an interest in international affairs will realise, is a very long way off to put it mildly. It is a war against direct enemies and also against indirect enemies, those who might just turn out to be enemies.

The significance of 'indirectness' may not be immediately apparent unless it is recalled that senior US officials such as Attorney-General John Ashcroft have made a habit of talking in very general terms about the nature of 'terrorism'. There are terrorists such as Osama Bin-Laden who threaten military action against the US; but what US officials like Ashcroft mean by 'terrorist' takes them well-beyond al-Qaeda. It takes them to all those who oppose 'American values' and the 'American ideal of liberty'. It takes them in the direction of those who oppose global capitalism. Whether the US administration will be able to extend the definition of terrorist to include those who oppose American interests in such fashion is unclear. What is clear, however, is that the climate is hardly favourable for the development of an anti-capitalist movement genuinely committed to far-reaching change. In some sense we have returned to the scenario described in chapter two where we discussed how the Cold War simplified politics to an Us and Them scenario that in turn served to mobilise opinion against radical initiatives. It seems clear that we have entered a new Cold War, one between the forces of 'civilisation' and the forces of 'terror' which may include those who are regarded as a threat to the American way of life. It is a difficult and dangerous time for anti-capitalists. But how exactly does such an externality impact in terms of options for the movement? It means that:

- A strategy that contemplated *direct confrontation* with US-backed interests or elites is a necessarily high risk one as a means of advancing anti-capitalist causes, the risk being intervention in the name of 'containment' of a potentially 'terroristic' development. This is particularly so in the case of revolutionary strategies of the classic 'putschist' kind; but it even affects electorally based strategies. The example of the left-wing Chilean president Salvador Allende, overthrown in a CIA-backed coup in 1973, is a reminder of what may lie ahead even for popularly elected – but radical – figures. This emphasises the desirability of 'popular' or 'united front' strategies between progressive political causes to undermine any strategy of 'containment', which by its nature seeks to *isolate* 'hostile' forces.
- Given the overwhelming military and police capacity available to advanced capitalist countries, the *open, predictable and symmetrical* use of force against the state is unlikely to prove effective. Under such conditions a wide variety of tactics and measures, including covert, dispersed, concealed and confusing

actions, as well as direct action, is likely to be more productive. Strategies of non-violent resistance may also be effective under certain circumstances, but do not themselves *prevent* the use of state violence (as at Quebec where pacifist protesters were attacked). Nor does non-violence guarantee the success of progressive campaigns and causes, particularly where they challenge the deeply entrenched privileges of elites as opposed to querying specific injustices.

- It follows from the above that an anti-capitalist cause needs to advance 'hegemonically', that is, through challenging, querying, engaging with and winning over 'everyday' habits of thought and reasoning. As we noted in chapter three, events, carnivals and protests are expressly *educative* in this sense, designed to foster a 'critical mass' of engaged and aware individuals whose overwhelming numbers can act as a counter-force to repressive state action.

- Those who despair at the pivotal position of the US in global politics might look for comfort at the key role direct action and popular protest have played as forces for change in recent American history. They may also wish to reflect on the fact that some of the largest and most effective anti-capitalist protests, including those at Seattle and Washington (to name but two), took place in the US. Indeed, as Amory Starr's *Naming the Corporate Enemy* shows, in terms of scope, size and variety the US anti-capitalist (or anti-globalization/ neoliberal/corporate) movement is one of the most extensive, if not *the* most extensive in the developed world. From this point of view the pivotal position of the US might well become a source of *hope* for anti-capitalists as the movement gathers momentum.

the increasingly mobile nature of transnational capitalism

In earlier eras anti-capitalist strategies focused on taking back that which was wrongfully appropriated, particularly natural resources such as land or forests. As the industrial revolution swept throughout the modern world anti-capitalist resistances focused on the return of the means of production, on factories, mines and other physical plant where workers created 'value' for the capitalist. Now, it is said, capitalism creates value out of, in Charles Leadbetter's phrase, 'thin air'. What creates value is not so much the plant or workers producing a given physical object as the ideas or knowledge that went into its creation. The value of, for example, a piece of software lies much less with the means by which it is bought, sold and installed on a PC than in the reams of code in which it is written. It is the code that is of overwhelming value, and that code could be written by a suitably skilled employee anywhere in the world. At its most advanced capitalism is said to be 'liquid' both in terms of the conditions under which technological innovations are pursued and as regards capital itself: where things are made and under what conditions. Capitalists are indifferent to considerations of locale, of employment needs, or issues of relative development; indifferent not because they *want* to be, but because in their own self-perception they *have* to be indifferent to such considerations to compete 'effectively'. It is for this reason that we have seen over the past thirty years a constant acceleration of the growth, development and collapse of industries, production, innovation. Capitalists pride themselves on *generating* 'liquidity': it is what they thrive on. Capitalism encircles the globe in an ever-increasing vortex of money, ideas, executives, plant, software. This has led many commentators (including those on the left) to conclude that the prospect for the development of any kind of radical alternative to capitalism must be poor to nonexistent. Contemporary capitalism is too fluid or elusive to be subject to political forces. How (if at all) do such considerations act as a constraint on contemporary anti-capitalist resistances?

- Local economies are increasingly subject to *capital flight*, meaning that banks and other major investors are able to shift money and resources around more quickly than ever, causing great hardship for local populations and often confrontation with local and national capital. But it is important not to confuse capital flight with the *flight of productive resources*, as if fields, mines and factories could disappear out of sight as fast as money invested in a stock exchange. Capital flight results in hardship where the *structure* of existing property holdings is left intact. Where such resources are reappropriated (as in some parts of Argentina, Brazil and Mexico) the condition of local inhabitants often *improves*.
- The *transnationalisation of capital* does not itself obviate the importance of production or the productive process for creating value. Whether a factory is located in Indonesia or the US, it remains a factory and thus potentially of use for alternative

forms of production and exchange. That 'innovative ideas' are mobile is not the same as saying that they are incapable of being harnessed for not-for-profit purposes either. Nor does it imply that the means of turning them into products ceases to be critical to capitalist enterprises. Far from surviving on 'thin air', capitalism relies on a vast reserve army labouring away in factories and mines, on the land and in the forests. That the productive process has been rendered 'invisible' to many in the North does not mean that production has somehow ceased to exist, or indeed that it has become less central to our lives. Production goes on, just as it always has, and thus the classic question, 'who gets what, when, where and how' remains just as relevant now as it did at any time in the past.

- Local, regional, even 'statist' anti-capitalist strategies are not rendered irrelevant by the transnationalisation of capital. It is perhaps more demanding to avoid hardship for local populations in the event that such strategies become the basis for national policies, as for example in Cuba. However, most Cubans are hardly worse off in *material* terms than ordinary people living in many other states in Latin America, despite the fact that Cuba lies outside the 'world system'.

from here to there: movement dynamics and collective action

Even considering the difficulties posed by the externalities, the most vexatious issue confronting the anti-capitalist movement of movements is deciding how it should develop. What should be obvious is that there are a number of what are termed 'fault lines' running through the movement which prevent its immediate coalescence around a political programme. I have in the course of the text focused on two: the reformism/radicalism fault line and the ideological/non-ideological fault line, but there are a number of others that we have alluded to in the course of our brief unpacking of the various anti-capitalist positions. Most noticeable are the fault lines between the North and the South. This is to say that there exists a very definite tension, sometimes ideologically-based and sometimes more intuitively-felt, between the demands of those from wealthy countries and those from poorer countries. Sometimes this

is expressed almost in terms of the South not wishing to be patron-
ised by northern NGOs who are 'caring' for their interests. Or it
might be in terms of the moral superiority that some northern
observers see in radical groups of the South such as the Zapatistas or
Sem Terra, who in turn say they have little to learn from the experience of those from outside the South. There are other 'faultlines' as
well. It has been noticeable that the radical feminist critique of the
'masculine' languages or an either/or position vis-à-vis 'reform or
revolution', has made advances, in turn fuelling the suggestion that
the movement requires 'feminising' or indeed that 'leadership'
should be handed over to women activists who in some sense are
better able to develop non-confrontational ways of developing the
movement. And we could go on to explore the tensions between the
various kinds of grouping, that is between NGO-driven activism,
direct action activism, or more conventional party-based activisms
as well. Some of these fault lines are more disabling than others.
Some, that is, seem to be a genuine obstacle to collective action and
others seem much less so. Of the two fault lines we have been
concentrating on here, the reformism/radicalism divide has received
far more attention than the ideological/non-ideological divide. This
is to say that many commentators are aware of and more concerned
about the lack of commonly agreed ends and goals than they are
about the way in which political demands or visions are developed
and articulated.

Having now unpacked some of the better known positions
within the anti-capitalist movement, it should by now be evident
that the reformism/radicalism divide is a serious one. But it is hardly
fatal. Political radicals can and always have worked alongside
'reformists' in the past. How? Quite simply because radicals have
always hoped that they will be able to radicalise their 'partners' or
that events will in some sense conspire to radicalise moderates for
them. Political opportunism and the capacity to adapt has often
been an important part of the radical outlook, particularly the
outlook of Marxists, helping them to cope with the 'barren times',
whilst preparing them for the openings to come as growth falters. It
should be recalled that what has gone for the 'red' camp has also
gone for the 'green', particularly in countries with a radical green
tradition. In Germany, for example, the advance of greens as a
serious political force is marked by the pendulum-like movement
between the reformists or 'realos' and radicals or 'fundis'. Yet
somehow they conspire to live under the same 'roof', each side aware

of the problem of pursuing their discrete vision from outside the 'mainstream'.

Thinking about the dynamics of the global anti-capitalist movement it is from this point of view not inconceivable that reformers and radicals will be able to paper over some of their differences by agreeing to what the latter will call a 'transitional' programme. This would be an essentially social democratic programme with a necessarily green tinge. It would, that is, leave the basic structures of global capitalism intact whilst calling for marginal or moderate reforms of the system of global governance together with a degree of redistribution from North to South and all within a package of 'sustainable development'. Such a programme would satisfy relatively few within the movement, but there is a palpable impatience amongst leading commentators and activists for *some* sort of programme around which to group. Indeed many leading radicals are aware that impatience can have negative as well as positive consequences. A compromise or 'transitional' programme of this sort might look like this:

- Reform of global institutions permitting greater representation of currently under-represented groups and regions: the South, NGOs, WSF (the democratic element).
- 'Deglobalisation' of global trade; debt relief/abolition; 'fairer' trade agreements; ban on dumping of subsidised goods from North to South.
- Sustainable policies for development and trade using tariffs and protective measures against corporations that promote environmentally damaging forms of production.
- Global treaties to secure better working conditions on a universal basis. The end of child labour, sweatshop conditions, and the exploitation of women.
- Greater controls on the arms trade; better mediation of international conflicts; an enhanced forum for regional and global dialogue to resolve longstanding issues such as the Israeli/Palestinian dispute.

Such policies are unlikely to be found obnoxious in themselves to anti-capitalist activists. They are the progressive equivalent of 'motherhood and apple pie', which is to say that the measures are 'important' and 'significant' for reformers of the global system, acceptable palliatives for many radicals. On the other hand, it is important not to overstate the degree to which deep ideological divisions can be smoothed over in such fashion. Mere use of the term 'sustainable development' would be enough to disenchant many radical greens, for example, who regard such a concept as little more than an oxymoron whose 'true' meaning would be more like 'unsustainable market economy'. The more committed to a particular vision, the more idealistic groups and individuals are, the less they will feel inclined to join in this global clamour for a clear programme to advance the cause. So much seems only to be accepted. The point, nevertheless is that reformism/radicalism need not be as immobilising politically as might at first seem. One of the features of the current phase of anti-capitalist protest is the drumming up of a sense of 'urgency' to build a movement, and this urgency is for many greater than the necessity for maintaining a purity of belief or politics. What is novel in other words, is that many activists and commentators are more prepared than ever to get their hands 'dirty' thrashing out compromises in the search for some sort of consensus. With the political will, one person's radical reformism can become another person's 'transitionary programme'. With the same will, one person's quest for social justice can become another's 'united front' against the forces of neoliberalism. In such fashion radicals and reformers can and do work together, if perhaps only temporarily. They might not be working from the same premises, but they can sing from the same song sheet with an ardour and sense of purpose that even mainstream political parties would find difficult to match.

beyond ideology: logics of resistance

There is evidently considerable temptation amongst commentators and activists to assume that the division between radicals and reformers within the anti-capitalist movement must be the fundamental one, and thus that assuming that some form of compromise is possible, such divisions may be overcome. As I have suggested above, it is possible that such divisions may indeed be overcome, if only temporarily. But they will not overcome the division between those who think that anti-capitalism is best confronted with an alternative ideological project and those who think that 'ideological projects' – and not just of the neoliberal variety – are part of the problem to be overcome. It would be wrong, on the other hand, to think that there is no awareness of the problem. Far from it, prominent writers have forcefully articulated their fears for a movement that is corralled into acceptance of a given ideological line or analysis. Naomi Klein has argued eloquently that what gives the movement its strength is precisely the fact that it *lacks* a line or ideology of the sort we have been discussing. Yet in her more recent writings she – like many others – has become preoccupied with a fear of the powerlessness or ineffectuality that the lack of a clear position implies. Paul Kingsnorth in his account of the global anti-capitalist movement, *One No, Many Yes*, is rather more specific in his critique, documenting the ways in which the British SWP attempts to annex anti-capitalist protests as a recruiting ground for their own very particular anti-capitalist 'vision'. He notes with some regret that at a time when regions and countries have been encouraged to form their own social forums to link up to the WSF, many in the UK are loath to do so for fear that it will quickly become an outpost of the SWP. Such fears are not confined to individuals such as Klein and Kingsnorth, but resound around the activist base of the movement in the UK and elsewhere. The direct action grouping *Schnews* went so far as to publish a pamphlet *Monopolise Resistance* 'outing' the anti-capitalist initiative 'Globalise Resistance' as an SWP 'front'. What is implicit in the criticisms is that anti-capitalism is 'larger' than any one ideology or any grouping can make it. Thus the reduction of the anti-capitalist movement to one vision will inevitably exclude some and alter its character in negative ways.

What the comments of Klein and Kingsnorth illustrate is the difficulty of thinking through alternatives to conventional forms of political organisation, particularly the Leninist Party. It is for this reason that their analysis is imbued with *anticipatory regret* about what the anti-capitalist movement will become at the hands of 'professional' politicians and activists, and all this before it has actually 'happened'. They like some things as they are, but, as it is, the anti-capitalist movement seems to be 'going nowhere'. In Klein's own analysis the anti-capitalist movement seems, like a scratched record, to be stuck in a form of 'serial protesting'. It has become a spectacle, its positive achievements disturbingly few and far-between. The rulers rule, the poor get poorer, and nothing very much seems to change. Paradoxically, Klein's lament echoes that of Alex Callinicos, one of the best known SWP activists. In his view the movement suffers from 'movementism' – even shorter hand for 'serial protesting'. Movementism equates to the view that merely by protesting or blockading important gatherings, significant blows are delivered to the structure of global capitalism, and thus what is needed are more and ever larger protests. In his view no such damage is inflicted, yet the persistent belief that it *is* prevents the movement from seeing that it is only by creating a counter-power in the form of a broad mass party that real changes can be argued for and won. Klein may not agree with the prescription, yet her own analysis remains suggestive rather than persuasive – as she willingly admits. Yet, as is obvious, both Klein and Kingsnorth articulate the fears of many. After all, at the first World Social Forum in 2001 official political parties and organisations were banned from the main sessions, thereby excluding not only Marxist parties, but also the Zapatistas. Is there no choice, no other way in which the movement could develop without tearing itself apart?

Without wanting to over complicate it, what the discussion shows is that there is a further fault line to be considered: one between those who wish to see the anti-capitalist movement develop into a *conventional political organisation* and those who wish to see it maintain and build upon its *disaggregated, dispersed and decentred* character. For the sake of a shorthand term to describe these competing notions we will term the former *the logic of 'majoritarian' politics* and the latter *the logic of 'minoritarian' politics*.

To fill this out further, in the anti-capitalist movement we find those who argue that the immediate task is to confront global capitalism with an *alternative system*, one that works for the benefit of the many as opposed to the few. This implies coalescence around a programme, the establishment of a leadership, a formal organisation of a movement of party type, a strategy for capturing power and for changing the existing order in accordance with the programme. The logic of 'majority' politics thus presupposes the elaboration of vertical relations between those at the top of the movement – those who lead, and those at the bottom – those who follow. To permit the top to be controlled, influenced or made answerable to the membership below, such structures presuppose the elaboration of systems of representation and accountability.

A minoritarian logic explicitly repudiates the need or desirability for an alternative 'system'. It rejects the need for a programme, typically in favour of direct action coordinated through alliances and coalitions of 'minorities'. It involves rejecting the idea of a movement or party-type structure, and thus the need for leadership, hierarchy, and bureaucracy in favour of what is sometimes termed '(dis)organisation', which is to say a form of organisation that is non-hierarchical, flat and easily remoulded in terms of shifting needs and priorities. It is a logic orientated towards action over representation, participation over command. Minority politics points towards *horizontal* political practices, and sees resistance as developing organically rather than strategically, that is, out of the immediate concerns felt by people and groups in particular locations.

It is clear that this fault line follows in approximate terms that between ideological and post-ideological politics. Most ideological politics is in the sense used here majoritarian; most minoritarian politics is post or non-ideological. But they do not map exactly on to each other. Some ideologically committed anarchists would favour a minoritarian politics (for example), and some – perhaps most – non-ideological reformists would favour a majoritarian politics built on conventional party structures. Let's try to unpack these logics to see where the strengths and weaknesses may lie in terms of the overall issue: what is/are the future(s) of anti-capitalism?

in search of the 'majority'

Most groups with clearly delineated accounts of what is wrong with the world and what is required to make the world better typically proceed with the elaboration of a *programme* or *manifesto* in which their analysis is framed and presented. A programme tells us about what the group represents or stands for, what its values are. It typically tells us how the world should be altered in accordance with these values and how it is that the programme should be realised. Of course there are very great differences between groups concerning what these values are, what sort of institutions should be promoted or protected, what kind of world is to be created or restored. Yet, whether radical or reactionary, an ideology or world view needs to be articulated; it needs to be presented so that people see what the group stands for. The programme is thus a means for mobilising people in support of the cause. In the first place it is designed to create a political organisation, either a loose movement or a more tightly constructed party. Hopefully it will get those who are broadly sympathetic to sign up for the cause by becoming members or affiliates, or by voting for them at elections.

The object of ideological politics is the *capturing of power* so that the programme can be enacted and put into practice. Once in power, the object is the *maintenance of power*. This is not to say that ideological politics is necessarily undemocratic politics; far from it. It is merely to note that the object of the political party or movement is to use power for the purpose of enacting a vision of the world in conformity with its values, or belief system, or idea about how the world should look. The *rationale* of the US Republican Party is the same as the rationale of the German Greens, despite the enormous differences in the *kind* of worlds they wish to construct. Not all parties or movements, however, are democratic or want to use the power available in liberal-democratic states to enact their vision. Most Marxist parties are not interested in seeking power on these terms because they are hostile to liberal-democratic politics as anything other than a means to the construction of a post-capitalist order. They are seeking to mobilise people to overthrow the established political system. But they still need to capture power in order to do so. Thus, to those with a clear project to accomplish, an *effective* politics is one that is able to articulate itself in the form of a programme or manifesto that will then mobilise support behind its cause. This will provide the basis for capturing power, whether through elections or through some moment of 'seizure'. Once in power the programme then needs to be enacted which in turn implies maintaining power. In liberal democratic states this is achieved through re-election – preferably 'serial' re-election. In other kinds of political system this might be through plebiscite, or referenda or single-party elections. How do these observations map onto the discussion of anti-capitalism?

There are many within the anti-capitalist movement who argue for an elaboration of a politics of this kind. The problem with the anti-capitalist movement is that it is not a *movement* as the term is normally understood. It lacks a programme or manifesto or ideology stating what it is *for* as opposed to what it is *against*. As we have already remarked, it lacks movement or party 'characteristics'. This is to say that it doesn't have any identifiable leaders. There is no permanently staffed office that could begin raising funds, organising members, producing literature, lobbying organisations, preparing spokespeople, and running for elections. This is, evidently, a source of immense frustration for many. How, they ask, can the anti-capitalist movement be *effective* if it is not constituted as a movement? Since 1999 there has been a great stampede to get out manifestos and programmes for change, each jostling for our attention, each proclaiming its superiority in terms of offering an analysis of the present; each portraying with varying skill and conviction the better world to come. 'Another world is possible!' Yes, if only it were *my* world, *my* vision, *my* values that everyone accepted as valid. If only the loose movement of movements could become a more tightly knit movement (period), then it could advance the cause of justice and democracy for all. What those who would like to see such a change are signalling is that to be effective, the anti-capitalist movement needs a programme or manifesto. It needs to build a party or movement proper out of the movement of movements. It needs to capture power within existing states so as to build an organisation or structure such as a global state better able to bring about progressive demands. Then it needs to maintain this new system in being against the neoliberals or corporations. Political energies thus need to be focused and sharpened for the struggles to come. The current movement is too diffuse, too disparate; it cannot capture 'the system' and transform it into something else – the *better* world people so crave.

Majoritarian politics thus necessitates '*vertical*' *political practices.* A political organisation is on this view a hierarchical structure. It requires *leadership*, *direction*, and *organisation*. It requires clearly stated *goals* that can be articulated by *representatives* of the organisation. A political organisation is often in this sense a 'government in waiting' even if – as in the case of some ultra-radical groups – it is unprepared to 'wait' to be elected into power as per liberal-democratic politics. It sees the state as a means for projecting its view of how the world should look onto society. Lacking these characteristics will make the organisation ineffective and thus unable to achieve its ends. What should be emphasised is that, like states, political organisations can be more or less democratic. This is to say that the means by which leaders are made accountable to the membership can be more or less open and dynamic. Some party systems are highly undemocratic, others are much more so. Radical groups often utilise all sorts of means to ensure that this democratic accountability is effective, sometimes at the cost – so some would argue – of its appeal or effectiveness to the wider electorate. European green parties, for example, have typically refused to nominate or elect a single leader for precisely this reason, preferring instead to identify two or more spokespeople to represent the party to the media and the broader electorate. They want to show that they are against leadership cults, the build up of power in the upper echelons of the party and hence that they are serious about democracy. Yet greens are not hostile to vertical practices as such. As with most political parties their own view of political effectiveness rotates around the necessity for leadership, organisation and representative structures. Even green parties have a top and bottom, and thus a gap between those who 'lead' and those who 'follow'; between those who represent and those who are represented. The gap may not be as great as appears in traditional conservative or social democratic parties, some of which – like the British Conservative Party – have only recently introduced elections for the leadership of the party. Nonetheless, the gap is there for a purpose: to ensure that the party remains 'effective' and unconstrained by 'excessive' periods of consultation, which in turn hamper the development of a clear set of policies. No doubt a majoritarian anti-capitalist movement would be more like the German Green party than the British Conservative party. This is to say that leaders would strive to be accountable and democratic in the way they go about drawing up the programme, consulting members, and involving people in its activities on a day-to-day basis. But the point is, there will be leaders and then there will be the rest, the 'led'. Once in power, there will be those who govern and those who are governed.

What then are the strengths and weaknesses of this approach in terms of the development of anti-capitalism? In terms of the strengths, those who defend the need to move in this direction do so on the following terms:

- In order to mobilise large numbers of people, *clear goals and objectives* are required. Political movements cannot be successful unless people know what they stand for. The development of a programme is needed to prevent the movement becoming inchoate and unfocused, which in turn leads to disenchantment and powerlessness. The discussion will likely be on-going and permanent and involve wide consultation ensuring that the 'many' have their full say in terms of what goes into the programme.
- In order to 'change the world' a movement needs *power*. Without power, anti-capitalism remains a set of protests; with power, real action can be taken to alter the structure of global capitalism. The creation of a global anti-capitalist alternative necessitates capturing power, initially at the national level. It thus requires – in the case of advanced democratic states – an electoral as well as 'united front' strategy to gain power. Once a number of states have anti-capitalist or anti-corporate governments, blocs and alliances between states can be used to put pressure on global elites for the

construction of institutions of global governance, which could in turn be used to construct an alternative to neoliberal globalisation.

- A democratic structure is *accountable* to the needs and interests of the members of the movement, just as a democratic state or community remains subject to the needs and interests of its citizenry. This requires a clear institutionalisation of mechanisms of representation, accountability and transparency, such as rotation of office or the election of officials.

Why are many activists and commentators worried about the development of an anti-capitalist organisation in the sense outlined here? They argue:

- Anti-capitalism contains diverse and conflicting accounts of how the world should look, and how global capitalism should be resisted. Any move to develop a single programme will inevitably end up *excluding* elements within the movement who do not agree with it, thereby weakening the movement *as* a movement. A commitment, for example, to the creation of a global state would alienate the very many anarchists, autonomists, environmentalists and 'localisers' who are hostile to the further development of structures of global governance.
- The history of movements and parties shows that the goal of attaining power has *deleterious consequences* for the movement as a whole. In particular, it involves *compromises* and thus the constant *moderation* of political demands. This is particularly so where the movement or party concentrates on gaining power through election. The logic of elections pushes the political leadership towards policies acceptable to corporate-owned media and the 'middle-ground' generally.
- Vertically organised structures like parties and states endorse a formal separation of 'leaders' and 'led'. They thus mirror in form the unequal distribution of power and advantage that many within the anti-capitalist movement seek to challenge in their critiques of neoliberal globalisation. Anti-capitalism is an essentially *participatory* movement. It is one based on equality of 'voice'. Representative structures are *inconsistent* with the *form* of the anti-capitalism movement.
- As a radical movement anti-capitalism represents a threat to existing interests at local and global level, particularly corporate interests. Vertically structured parties and movements are much

more easily monitored and combated by forces that are hostile to their aims, goals, and values. In particular, movements with clearly defined leadership structures can be easily neutered through surveillance, arrests, and (in the last resort) assassination. Given the immense resources available to modern capitalist states, vertical structures can never be the basis for a genuinely transformative politics because they will always be 'outgunned' in electoral terms by parties backed by a pro-capitalist media and corporate sponsorship.

minoritarian logics – towards better world(s)

Tempting as it is to think that an effective politics requires vertical political practices, and that a movement of movements must be translated into a movement or party with a clear programme and a strategy for capturing power, such a politics is not all there is. Any account of the dynamics of anti-capitalism would be incomplete if it did not cover alternatives to the logic of majoritarianism. There is enough disquiet about the remorseless logic behind the calls for 'effectiveness', not only from commentators such as Klein and Kingsnorth but also from activists (as evidenced in activist literature and bulletin boards), that some consideration of the issue is required. In particular we need to focus on the demand that the current diffuse, disaggregated *form* of the anti-capitalist movement be in some sense mirrored in a *strategy* for confronting neoliberal globalisation. How in short could the shifting, plural, diverse nature of the movement be safeguarded and promoted without at the same time rendering it politically futile or ineffective?

This is a demanding question and one to which few have been able to give a convincing answer. Nonetheless, it is a pressing issue for the anti-capitalist movement and requires some sort of response, if only to highlight that the majoritarian 'logic' is not the only one found within the movement. One way to think about this might be to turn the issue around and ask how it is that the movement has come to the position that it is now in. How is it that this dispersed, 'anarchic', free-flowing, 'leaderless' movement of movements has been able to operate at all? We might ask how 'it' has been able to mobilise hundreds of thousands of people at marches, demonstrations, sit-ins, occupations all around the world? How has it been able to put the fate of global capitalism on the agenda of world politics despite having none of the material resources available to states, mainstream political organisations, or the larger NGOs for that matter? How has it been able to get millions of people thinking, reflecting, wondering what comes 'next'? The answer is obviously not because the anti-capitalist movement is 'politically ineffectual'. Nor, however, is the answer because it is well led, with clear goals and objectives, or because it presents an attractive picture of a world to come. It cannot be any of these, because as we know, this is what the movement is said to *lack*. So what's left? What is it that makes people anti-capitalist/neoliberal/corporate? More specifically, what is it that makes people want to identify with something that lacks all those things that many commentators and activists seem to think are prerequisites for political identification? Surely the answer lies within the *form* of the movement itself? But what can this mean?

'network' activism: form and function

Those who can remember the discussion in chapter two about where the movement came from will have some inkling as to where 'minoritarian' activists have been looking for clues. What emerges is that part of the answer lies with the *kind* of interactions and exchanges facilitated by the internet. This is not the same as saying that the internet created a particular kind of activism; but the kinds of disaggregated and dispersed forms of activism we see emerging out of the post-68 realignment were greatly helped by the development of the internet and communications technology generally. What, rather, we remarked upon is that the internet gave those with access a presence and a voice. Activists and groups could interact with one another on a basis that did not require that they subordinate themselves or their causes to some external or overarching logic. People with different concerns, different issues, different causes, different views of the world can interact, exchange ideas and information without becoming subordinated to others. It is a form of combination without the need for compromise, agreement, reconciliation, without the need to establish a hierarchy of views, without the need to silence some for the overall 'good' or 'benefit' of the many. The internet allows a form of interaction at 'zero cost', if not literally, then in terms of the logic of 'normal' (i.e. majoritarian) political exchanges where, classically, 'compromise', 'give and take' and 'toeing the line' has been the norm ('my party, right or wrong').

The vast mushrooming of the use of the internet in activist circles is from this point of view hardly a surprise, but it also facilitates a vast extension of different 'activisms'. As we noted in chapter two, it encourages the elaboration and re-elaboration of activism in response to day-to-day events, a mobilisation of opinion, resources, direct action in the name of different, but intersecting causes and campaigns. It promotes temporary interchanges, interactions, alliances and coalitions against reactionary, regressive, or repressive actors. If part of the issue concerns how to mobilise people with very distinct problems, perspectives and politics then the internet has been as effective a *tool* of mobilisation as can ever have been utilised in the name of a cause. But effectiveness is not merely about mobilisation. It is also about changing policies, challenging elites, developing alternatives to neoliberal or corporate capitalism. How can such a dispersed form of activism be 'effective' on these terms?

The answer is not far from hand according to advocates. They point to a number of campaigns that have hampered, blocked or otherwise made difficult the life of corporate and global elites. These include most obviously the global campaign in support of the South Korean workers in the early 1990s and the mobilisation against the Multilateral Agreement on Investment (MAI), which was scuppered partly because of the feverish efforts of activists coordinated over the net. The case of the Zapatistas is also instructive in this respect in that the support of activists mobilised via the internet has been crucial to their survival, serving as a brake on the efforts of the Mexican government to launch an all-out war in the region. It is difficult not to conclude that the US's caution over how to deal with what is, after all, a revolutionary insurgency in its own 'back-yard' has something to do with the knowledge that this is perhaps the most intensely 'watched' and watched over progressive movement in the world. Both the Mexican and US political elites know they are not 'alone'. No one and no state is 'alone' any more. What the internet makes possible is an ever-expanding network of sympathisers, fellow-travellers and activists all linked, all separate, all 'equal', all capable of mobilising themselves in myriad ways to sometimes unpredictable effect. Looking at such examples it would be curious to conclude that the formless, leaderless, and just dispersed nature of internet-based activism is ineffective. Perhaps it is the very inchoate nature of this global (non)-alliance that gives it the power to block the actions of those who would in the past have barely hesitated before confronting militarily a poorly armed and equipped rebel force like the Zapatistas?

We need, however, to think past what the internet is, and on to what it *prefigures* in terms of the question before us: how should/can the anti-capitalist movement be politically effective in terms other than those associated with the development of formally constituted parties or movements? The internet did not *create* anti-capitalist activism; rather anti-capitalist activists *used* the internet as a means of connecting to others. It was a convenient tool by which activists could communicate with each other, but they can and do communicate by many other means as well. This is necessary because of the ease with which internet based communication can be monitored or thwarted by state intervention, by surveillance or by bullying ISPs into conformity with repressive legislation. What also needs to be borne in mind is that many activists in the developing world have little or no access to the internet or high technology equipment. This has not, however, prevented the mobilisation of peasants, the rural poor, and factory workers behind anti-capitalist initiatives – sometimes in vast numbers. Nonetheless, we can think of the internet as representing in *form* a kind of horizontal activism with the following attributes:

- An activism that is based on *networks* of self-avowed minorities, rather than on classic models of political organisation, principally, parties, movements and majorities. As we discussed above, a network does not require a bureaucracy, standing officers, leadership, or mechanisms of representation. Those who wish to 'speak' can do so unmediated by the needs and interests of a perhaps distant leadership intent on sending the 'right' signals to the electorate, to powerful states or global institutions.
- Networks can be *extended indefinitely* and in more than one or two dimensions. There is no limit on who or what can join the network. There is no 'membership' as such, just engagement. There is no brake, organisational, fiscal, or ideological on joining in – merely access to the network.
- Networks facilitate *temporary alliances, coalitions, agreements, events, interactions*. A network consists of chains of allegiance and intersection or what are sometimes called 'nodal points' where there is convergence for the purpose of acting in support of some group or cause.

'hubs and spokes' vs 'the rhizome'

From this point of view, Naomi Klein is nearly right when she describes contemporary anti-capitalist interactions as approximating 'hubs and spokes'. What she is trying to articulate is the sense in which the anti-capitalist movement is composed of separate-but-equal units that interact with each other rather than becoming agglomerated to some larger whole. The difficulty with the analogy should, however, be clear even from our brief discussion. 'Hubs and spokes' imply the necessity for a centre, the hub, to which everything else is connected. If there is a 'centre' of the anti-capitalist movement then 'it' can only be a temporary one, as for example in the form of the 'convergence' centres set up at various protests to facilitate the exchange of information, coordinate protests and demonstrations, print leaflets and so on. Or it is in the form of the social forums that act as temporary sites for discussion, lobbying and showpiece debates. Other than these highly contingent senses, it is surely obvious that this is a 'hub-less' movement. 'Hubs and spokes' is in addition too mechanical an analogy, implying that there is some fixed form of interaction between constituent elements, with fixed 'spacing' between groups and activists. Again, this is a curiously inapt way of thinking about activist combination and recombination, which is much more protean and free-form than these descriptions allow. But what kind of analogy *is* appropriate to describe the network as opposed to the party-in-waiting or the movement-which-isn't-a-movement?

A number of activists and commentators have made reference to the analogy of the 'rhizome' found in Deleuze and Guattari's *A Thousand Plateaus*, an otherwise hugely demanding philosophical work written towards the end of the 1970s. A rhizome is, they explain, composed of a perennial stem growing under the ground, shooting out roots in a random tangle. It contrasts with 'arborescent' plants that grow upwards from a single trunk or stem. In a rhizome leaves and flowers appear above the ground, so that we get the impression that there are separate plants growing in the same place. In fact all the 'separate' plants are connected to the same roots. Deleuze and Guattari use the 'rhizome' analogy in opposition to the idea of 'arborescence' to explore anti-systemic phenomena as opposed to 'statist' hierarchical phenomena. Now what intrigues people about the analogy is that it seems to encapsulate something of the *form* of the anti-capitalist movement. For some it also seems to suggest a way out of the puzzle described above concerning how it is that the movement can 'develop'. How so?

As regards the question of form, there are many 'visible' elements in the anti-capitalist movement, particularly the massive protests for example at Genoa, Prague and Quebec. Yet the charge that anti-capitalism has failed to get past 'serial protesting' or 'movementism' is one that discounts too easily that which cannot be 'seen' or which is less visible to the untutored eye. This is, in the case of Klein in particular, what she herself has been dramatically documenting: the massive increase in the level of grassroots activism of all shapes and

PRAGUE – WHAT HAPPENED?

After Seattle there was considerable curiosity amongst the activist community in Europe to see if the Seattle experience would be repeated. The omens were certainly promising. A May Day 'Carnival against Capitalism' in London had taken the authorities completely by surprise in terms of numbers and impact. A huge demonstration turned up in Vienna in January 2000 to protest against the Haider regime. At the end of June 60,000 activists turned up in Millau, France ('The Seattle of the Tarn') to show solidarity with farmers who had been arrested for trashing a McDonald's. A meeting of the IMF and World Bank in Prague in September provided the pretext for the first major post-Seattle European demonstration. The Czech police had obviously been 'well-briefed' and many thousands of heavily armoured police were waiting for the demonstrators. Here, however, the demonstration differed in significant ways to that of Seattle. Here too the diversity of groups and protests; but here also a greater co-ordination amongst groups and between groups, and the emergence of 'convergence' centres to arrange marches and actions. The protest was also noticeable for its international – not just European – flavour, with many delegations and groups from around the world. Heavy policing on this occasion made sure most of the official meetings took place, though anti-globalisation figures such as Walden Bello were invited by President Havel to address the assembled 'dignitaries'. Prague was also notable for the disaggregation of the protest itself, with different marches for different activist groups – and also for the attendance of many well-known figures from the newly emergent movement.

sizes, together with the huge spread of the network that often under-pins direct action. Yet this unseen part is precisely the element from which the protests, the visible part, springs. In the rhizome metaphor what is significant is not that which is 'visible' – in this case the televisual protests and carnivals of the oppressed – but that which is subterranean, 'below ground' and thus hidden from view. Whilst the protests might be *reminders* of the existence of a move-ment, they are not in this sense the movement itself. Rather, the movement is the network, the tangle of 'roots', that underpins the protests. Thus even assuming there were no further protests, there would in this view still be a movement, a network, and multiple forms of activism. All of this is far too developed to disappear through lack of opportunities to mount the large protests that have brought anti-capitalism to the forefront of the attention of the world's media. So 'anti-capitalism' is not simply about protests, and protests are not the measure of its effectiveness. So what is? What does the rhizome offer as a 'model' of political change?

Following through with the analogy, left to itself a rhizome will carry on growing until it crowds out everything else in the garden. It does it in a way that is 'unseen', that is, through the endless multipli-cation of shoots under the ground. Yet there comes a point where the rhizome occupies the entire space, where there is *nothing but* the network of roots and leaves multiplying and remultiplying. Transferring the analogy, we come to the idea sometimes termed the 'hollowing out' of neoliberal capitalism. Networks of resistance keep on multiplying, keep on growing and gaining supporters who mobilise each other in support of actions, individuals and groups confronting some aspect of capitalism. The idea is thus that the net-work supports, sustains and nourishes forms of interaction that resist and challenge the neoliberal occupants of the existing 'space'. This would not be in a 'linear' way as suggested in the classic move-ment or party model, but in a 'rhizomatic' way, in a way that is dri-ven by the particular needs, desires and ideas of those who compose the movement or network as opposed to those who 'represent' it. In this sense it would be more accurate to talk about the movement recovering spaces that have been lost ('the commons') and creating new spaces outside and beyond the control of elites, permitting people to reclaim that which is rightfully theirs/ours. This is by con-trast to the idea of 'building' a movement 'block' by 'block' which, once built, will *then* directly confront elites in a set piece 'battle' for political power.

This still leaves the question of political change and transformation. In the majoritarian model we can see quite clearly how change is said to be produced, even if many are sceptical about the scenario described. The story is so familiar that there is little difficulty in understanding how it *might* work, even if many are sure it won't – or won't in a sense that remains true to the nature of the anti-capitalist movement itself. A programme is constructed, power is captured, the world is 'changed,' and in the meantime those whose view of how the world fails to conform with the programme are left with the same feelings of powerlessness, alienation and exclusion as before – if perhaps with some compensations. How does a 'disorganisation' of the rhizomatic kind actually challenge existing power structures? How can neoliberalism be supplanted?

Again, the accent in this approach is not so much according to a strategy of 'capturing' power and changing 'the system' for some 'better', more 'rational' alternative. In models of disorganisation, it would be more accurate to talk about the system being 'by-passed', 'drained', or in some other fashion undermined from 'within' or 'below'. The Zapatistas for example claim that they are uninterested in 'capturing' power, only 'exercising' it. This is to say that what they reject is the idea of having to take power in classic 'organisational' terms, and *then* to use the power for the benefit of those represented. What they have sought, rather, is to secure the means by which the indigenous peasants can exercise control over their own lives. It was still a prerequisite in the case of the Zapatistas that the Chiapas region was 'secured', a reminder that any politics has of necessity a *spatial* dimension, even an avowedly 'minoritarian' politics. Space, resources, capacities have to be won back, creating a different space of possibility. In the case of the Zapatistas the 'space' had to be secured militarily in order for the peasants to be empowered at all. Obviously, in many parts of the world the military occupation of space is hardly relevant – not yet in any case. But it is less the *way* in which space was occupied and more that the space itself was transformed from being a setting in which things *happened to* people, to one in which what happens is *subject to* people 'exercising' power. For minoritarian activists this is a key point: what is important is the 'local' contextualised setting in which actions take place. For them it matters that strategies are developed by the people for whom they are intended to benefit; that representative structures are avoided in favour of participatory ones; that communities run their own affairs; that 'leadership' – if it exists – is one based on 'listening' rather than speaking. This is not a template for political action as such, and few would regard it as being so. It is an attempt to escape from the majoritarian logic described above: the logic of ideology, manifestos, representation, and vertical structures. It is an escape from 'politics' as this has long been practiced and thought about over the past two millennia.

The example of the Zapatistas reminds us of the availability of horizontal political structures, difficult though it is to dislodge the fixation many within the anti-capitalist movement have for developing vertical ones. Horizontal structures are essentially *networks* composed of individuals, groups and activisms that relate to one another in non-hierarchical, non-subordinating ways. In a horizontal setting voices are *distinct and equal.* This is what the Zapatistas mean when they say that their orientation is to seek 'dignity' and 'respect' for the people living in the Chiapas. The aim is to listen rather than legislate. On horizontal terms, political action is facilitated through *coalition and alliances*, rather than through 'building' a party or movement. This is to say that the individual molecules or groups composing the network retain their distinct identity, character, ends and goals, *even whilst* acting with others. Alliances and coalitions are contingent, temporary arrangements. This is not to say that they cannot be long-lasting, only that they can be brought to an end by groups at any time for whatever reason. In this sense the 'united front' strategy which has been seen in the course of the twentieth century, particularly with respect to combating fascism, is one example of a horizontal mechanism of political action. For those who argue for the necessity of 'building' vertical structures the united front can only be at best a halfway house towards an organisation ('the Party') that is 'genuinely' capable of confronting entrenched forces. But for those concerned about maintaining the distinctiveness of the individual parts of the movement of movements, the united front notion at least has the virtue of retaining the integrity of the component parts. Horizontal political forms also imply highly contingent social, economic and political solutions. Just as party and movement structures are anathema in this political logic, so too are state-like structures, as they dilute or deny the capacity of individuals and groups to combine and recombine on mutual terms. What this similarly implies is a massive 'deglobalisation' of power away from institutions and permanent structures towards the 'molecules' whose actions combine to constitute the field of social, economic and political life.

Advocates of a minoritarian approach and horizontal political structures argue that its strengths are as follows:

* The anti-capitalist movement is *already* 'disorganised' and 'minoritarian'. Whatever successes it has enjoyed so far in terms of mobilising people is due to the fact that it refuses to conform to the logic of conventional political organisations. This implies that it is an essentially *inclusive* form of politics that permits the widest range of interests, views and ideologies to co-mingle for mutual support and aid without threatening to submerge these differences in an over-arching programme or structure that necessarily excludes some for the name of the greater good of the 'whole'.
* Power needs to be *drained away* from politicians, representatives and institutions so that people are able to exercise power over their own lives without subordinating or dominating others. This is to say that power has to be used 'creatively' to support and maintain horizontal relationships. The attempt to construct anti-capitalism as a fully-fledged movement or party is to embark on a road at the end of which lies the same macro-political structures that have served the peoples of the world, particularly the developing world, so poorly. It is a recipe for the abstraction of power to the wealthy, the articulate, the establishment, to the new 'elite'. A 'minor' politics insists that changing the 'masters' does not get rid of the 'masters' or the 'slaves'.
* Democratic institutions enshrine the necessity for 'leaders' and 'led', and thus the need for mechanisms of accountability and control against the abuses of power that such relationships imply. A 'disorganised' network has no need for such mechanisms as the terms and conditions upon which combination take place are contingent and 'permanently impermanent'. Whatever institutions and structures exist to regulate relations between and within networks are *subject to* those networks and the members of them, rather than the other way around.
* A network lacking hierarchies, leaders and permanent structures is much more difficult to contain by forces antithetical to the movement as a whole. Attacking one part of the network is not fatal to it. As a rhizomatic structure the anti-capitalist network resists efforts at its control, subordination or elimination by such forces. As with the rhizome, cutting off one of its 'heads', suppressing it in one location, attempting to control its spread through counter-insurgency methods will be largely

ineffective. The 'plant' will continue to grow across three dimensions, emerging at intermittent points to varying effect.

It goes without saying that just as there are critics of logic of majoritarian politics, so the supporters of the latter are equally critical of a minoritarian politics. They argue the following:

- The history of radical social movements shows that whilst 'spontaneous' energies are the key to the development of such movements, they cannot be effective in these terms. *Some* leadership and some *strategy* is required to ensure that radical energies do not dissipate under pressure of conformity or from the attentions of powerful states and anti-radical forces. There is a general recognition from *within* the anti-capitalist movement that some institutionalisation of the movement is required if it is not to wither on the vine of its own expectations. The proliferation of social forums is a sign of this, as is the attempt by umbrella groupings such as ATTAC and the Brazilian PT to get the movement as a whole to agree on a minimum programme that can unify progressive forces and serve as a launch pad for more radical measures as the movement is emboldened.
- The power of global elites is intensifying with the penetration of transnational capital into domestic economies. Localised actions cannot drain power from elites. Only coordinated action designed to confront global elites can be effective as a form of resistance. Power is a resource to be used to the benefit of the poor and oppressed until such time as they are able to help themselves. Many are unable to 'exercise' power because of chronic poverty, lack of educational means, political 'illiteracy' or cultural prejudices that have served to disable individuals as actors in their own rights. Power thus has to be used in the interim to recover the capacity of individuals to act for themselves.
- Disorganised 'structures', whether in the form of groups or networks, leave open the possibility for the development of what Jo Freeman in the context of the women's movement termed the 'tyranny of structurelessness'. Without institutions, rules and defined procedures guaranteeing that diverse opinions, positions and interests are represented, individuals and groups are prey to 'tacit' domination by the well-meaning but overbearing. 'Structurelessness' distorts outcomes in favour of the loudest, best organised or most radical groups, none of which may be necessarily representative of the feelings or opinions of the

individuals and groups contained within the movement as a whole. The result is likely to be the dissipation of radical energies in the mutual recrimination and mistrust that often accompanies such scenarios.

- Network activism may have the virtue of being difficult to track, but this is a correlate of it being 'leaderless' and thus unable to give direction during times of stress or crisis when opportunities present themselves for political advances. At such moments, great strides *can* be made by radical movements, but only if they are able to *act*. Network activism makes a fetish of communication at the expense of action, which in turn is only possible where there are people who are prepared to act in a coordinated way and in terms of an agreed strategy *for* action. Network activism assumes that people cannot act on a common front against a common enemy, and this is a recipe for *inaction*.

conclusion(s)

It is not difficult to discern that the arguments could (and do) go bouncing back and forth between individuals and groups identifying with one or other view of how the anti-capitalist movement should develop. As is apparent, the differences are fundamental, perhaps more fundamental than the other faultlines we have been considering. The differences are not just about the means, but more importantly about what kind of entity the anti-capitalist movement is to be, and beyond that about what kind of future the movement should and should not be building. One logic points towards coalescence of opinion around an alternative system to that of neoliberal capitalism. It points to the extension of the logic of modernity itself: a world in which equality and liberty have been attained for all, in which harmony reigns, in which enlightened representatives/planners/fellow citizens govern in the best interests of the governed. The other logic points towards a multiplicity of alternative systems and (non-)systems interconnected (perhaps), but separate and equal. It is a logic that implicitly challenges the notion articulated above: that there can be one world, one system, one set of relationships that are identifiably better, more just, more harmonious than a multitude of others. It is a logic that insists that the task of an anti-capitalist movement is not to determine the nature of the world to be created; merely to establish that *worlds* other than the neoliberal variety are possible. It is to insist that it is for people to determine for themselves how and under what terms they will live together; not to have such issues determined *for* them either by capitalists or, indeed, by benevolent souls possessed by a vision of a new and better world. The 'major'/'minor' debate is thus over the soul of globalisation, over global development, over what kind of future is to be created, on whose terms, for what ends.

Yet it would be wrong at the same time to imply that these dilemmas are new or somehow unique to the anti-capitalist movement. They are in essence the same tensions as those we find in every political movement or party that has ever existed. Every movement is made up of discrete parts, namely people, who have their own needs, wants and desires, some of which are 'present' in the aims and goals of a movement and some of which are not. Which party member or member of a movement has been able to say that the party or movement literally embodies every need, want or desire that they possess? Only the marionette-like stooges manipulated by power-hungry despots for their own cynical ends. For everyone else, political activity is usually a question of being prepared to see other people's points of view, to enter into pacts, alliances, coalitions and arrangements in the name of advancing *against* something as well as *towards* something we believe in. This is not to say that we are condemned to acting in instrumental or utilitarian ways, but that we are capable as 'political' animals of weighing up the relative importance of different courses of action in the name of advancing a cause. It sometimes means giving some things up and sometimes standing firm despite being in the 'minority'. As the political philosopher Hannah Arendt observed, we are *all* in this very particular sense, 'beginners'. We 'begin', rather than blindly follow. We initiate, we invent, we create and recreate; we think, calculate, observe, and of course we *act*, or rather we are capable of acting – if only we were given the chance.

The suspicion must be that the future of the anti-capitalist movement will depend upon many millions of 'beginnings' of this kind. It will be dependent upon many millions of individuals and groups deciding that they will act together to confront the Thing that they have all in their own manner, by different ways and means, decided must be resisted: neoliberal capitalism. How far they are prepared to go to challenge capitalism is the stuff of speculation, not analysis and description, which is what I have attempted to limit myself to here. What is clear is that the future is uncertain. That it is *uncertain* is, however, testimony to the *success* of the anti-capitalist movement in reintroducing history, contingency, morality and the importance of acting back into global politics where once it seemed impossible. It would therefore be quite mistaken to imply that the anti-capitalist movement has not *already* come a long way or that it has achieved little of significance. Let us not forget that Francis Fukuyama's article 'The End of History?', which provided the backdrop to the discussion in chapter two, was published in 1989. That article suggested that an overwhelming consensus had been reached about the nature of the world to come and that liberal-democracy, the political form of global capitalism, was unquestionably the hegemonic ideal of the new millennium. History was at an 'end', and 'certainty' reigned. Few mainstream commentators or analysts dared to contradict him back then – try as they might to muster reasons why he *might* be wrong. Within ten years that argument had itself been consigned to the dustbin of history together with the collective vanities of the world's elites now jolted out of the warm certainties outlined by Fukuyama. The 'impossible' fall of communism had been followed by the impossible fall of 'liberal-democracy' as unquestioned ideal for the end of history. It will be interesting to see how many other 'impossibilities' fall by the wayside through the efforts of 'anti-capitalists' to find and build 'another world' – or indeed other *worlds*.

resources

read on

Anon., 'A16 Revolutionary Anti-Capitalist Bloc Statement', www.infoshop.org/news5/a16_call.html

Alex Callinicos, 'Regroupment, Realignment and the Revolutionary Left', www.swp.org.uk/INTER/regroupen.pdf

Noam Chomsky, *9/11* (London: Seven Stories Press, 2001).

Harry Cleaver, 'The Chiapas Uprising and the Future of Class Struggle in the New World Order', www.eco.utexas.edu/facstaff/Cleaver/chiapasuprising.html

Gilles Deleuze and Felix Guattari, *A Thousand Plateaus* (London: Athlone Press, 1988 [1980]).

David Graeber, 'The New Anarchists', *New Left Review*, no. 13, Jan./Feb. 2002. Online at: www.newleftreview.net/NLR24704.shtml

Jo Freeman, 'The Tyranny of Structurelessness', www.jofreeman.com/joreen/tyranny.htm

John Holloway, *Change the World Without Taking Power: The Meaning of Revolution Today* (London: Pluto Press, 2002).

Naomi Klein, 'What's Next? in *Fences and Windows* (London: Flamingo, 2002).

Tom Mertes, 'Grass-Roots Globalism', *New Left Review*, no. 17, Sept./Oct. 2002. Online at: www.newleftreview.net/NLR25106.shtml

Robert Michels, *Political Parties: A Sociological Study of the Oligarchical Tendencies of Modern Democracy* (New York: Transaction 1998 [1911]).

Emil Sader, 'Beyond Civil Society: The Left after Porto Alegre', *New Left Review*, no. 17, Sept./Oct. 2002. Online at: www.newleftreview.net/NLR25105.shtml

Jean-Paul Sartre, *Critique of Dialectical Reason*, vol. 2 (London and New York: Verso, 1990).

James C. Scott, *Domination and the Arts of Resistance* (New Haven, CT: Yale UP, 1992).

Benedict Seymour, 'Nationalize This! What Next for Anti-Globalization Protests?', *Radical Philosophy*, May/June 2001. On line at: www.radicalphilosophy.com

Charles Tilly, *From Mobilization to Revolution* (Reading, MA: Addison-Wesley, 1978).

Leon Trotsky, *The New Course*, various editions, full text available online at: www.marxists.org/archive/trotsky/works/1923-nc/index.htm

link to

www.infoshop.org [contains a useful digest of alternative views on (dis)organization and horizontal activisms]

http://www.eco-action.org/dod/ [site for *Do or Die* – journal of eco-anarchism and direct action with articles on organisational issues]

www.schnews.org.uk [similar to above]

www.ruckus.org [non-violent direct action]

www.whitehouse.gov [latest on the war on terror/anticapitalism]

www.weareeverywhere.org

glossary of key terms, thinkers and movements

anarchism Umbrella term for all those who reject the need for a state or any other source of authority suspended above communities. Anarchists have also tended to reject the Marxian preoccupation with the revolutionary party and particularly with the idea of a revolutionary 'dictatorship of the proletariat' as the basis for creating a new order. Anarchists are suspicious of most claims to authority and regard ordinary people's capacity for self-organisation as a natural or desirable basis for any social order. Anarchism is otherwise a highly diverse tradition encompassing libertarians and individualists such as Max Stirner and Benjamin Tucker and collectivists (such as Pierre-Joseph Proudhon), syndicalists (Georges Sorel), anarcho-communists (Mikhail Bakunin, Alexander Berkman) and anarcho-feminists (Emma Goldman).

ATTAC *Association pour la Taxation des Transactions Financiéres pour L'aide aux Citoyens* [Association for the Taxation of Financial Transactions to Aid Citizens] created in France in 1998 under the auspices of the journal *Le Monde Diplomatique*, home to high profile figures such as Susan George, Bernard Cassen and Ignatio Ramonet. ATTAC picked up Nobel economist James Tobin's suggestion that a tax should be levied on the movement of capital out of financial markets, and used to support initiatives in the developing world. ATTAC is now itself an umbrella grouping with support networks across the world.

autonomism A hybrid of Marxism, anarchism and, depending on the particular 'tendency', several other currents of thought such as Situationism and environmentalism. Associated with the outright rejection of the state in favour of councils, soviets or other directly participatory forms of organisation. Accords primacy to 'class struggle' and the capacity of all people to organise themselves for the purpose of resistance and communal organisation. The best known autonomist thinker is Antonio Negri, author of *Time for Revolution* and (with Michael Hardt) of *Empire*.

Bové, José Associated with the *Confédération Paysanne* network based in France which seeks to protect and promote the rights of small landholders and agricultural workers across the world. High profile figure in France where he has been arrested on several occasions, most notably for trashing a McDonald's restaurant in his home town of Millau. Author of *The World is not for Sale*.

Chomsky, Noam (1928–) Professor of linguistics at the Massachusetts Institute of Technology (MIT), dissident and activist since the 1960s, and author of some of the best-known analyses of US foreign policy and global capitalism. These include: *Necessary Illusions: Thought Control in Democratic Societies*; *Rogue States: The Rule of Force in World Affairs*; *9/11*.

environmentalism Broad term covering all those who, in the wake of the growing awareness of the unsustainable nature of capitalism in the 1960s and 1970s, sought to promote forms of life that respected the 'limits to growth'. Within environmentalism there are two main currents: eco-centric approaches that favour preservation of the Earth over other considerations; and anthropo-centric approaches that seek sustainable, more or less industrialised forms of society. Well known figures include Murray Bookchin, John Zerzan and Dave Foreman, founder of Earth First!.

international monetary fund (IMF) Working closely with the World Bank, the idea of the IMF was to provide financial assistance and expertise to developing and developed countries thereby helping them to invest in the infrastructure needed to promote economic growth and stability. In practice assistance tends to come with many strings attached, including enforced cut-backs on welfare spending, and public sector deficits in turn cutting budgets for health, housing and education. Focus for protests because of the perceived manner in which public sector initiatives are sacrificed to business in the name of increased 'efficiency'.

Marx, Karl (1818–1883) Greatest anti-capitalist thinker of the modern age. Author (often with Friedrich Engels) of some of the classic works examining capitalism, the nature of historical development, revolution and post-capitalism. These include:
The Communist Manifesto, the three volumes of *Capital* and the *Grundrisse*.

marxism The doctrine or philosophy held by Marxists. However, 'Marxism' is itself an umbrella term for the numerous competing currents and tendencies such as Leninism, Trotskyism and Maoism that have sought to further refine Marx's work for practical purposes. Marxism emphasises the centrality of class struggle to revolutionary change and the necessity for the abolition of the market and the private ownership of the means of production. It also posits an ideal end point, 'communism', as distinct from 'socialism' which is regarded as a 'transition' period leading to communism.

neoliberalism In terms of ideas, neoliberalism represents the reassertion of the classical liberal concern to promote the maximum possible liberty and/or the maximum possible economic efficiency. In terms of politics, neoliberalism is associated with the rise to power of Mrs Thatcher in the UK and Ronald Reagan in the USA. However, in the 1970s and 1980s neoliberalism quickly established itself as the ideology 'of choice' for global elites generally, and the institutions of global governance such as the IMF more particularly. Neoliberalism in the contemporary context is asserted through the requirement to open markets and services to competition, to rein back public spending, and to endorse the commodification of the global 'commons', e.g. through gene patenting.

President 'Lula' da Silva Leader of the Brazilian Workers Party, and since 2002 President of Brazil. Host for the first three World Social Forums held at Porto Alegre, itself a centre for anti-capitalist initiatives and experiments (e.g. the idea of a 'participatory budget'). A 'national internationalist' who came to power promising the radical reform of Brazil, but without antagonising the IMF or major international investors.

Sem Terra *Movimento dos Trabalhadores Rurais Sem Terra* (MST) – The Brazilian Landless Workers Movement set up in 1985. Seeks to reappropriate unused farmland for use by peasants. The land is usually farmed cooperatively, with profits shared amongst the workers. Members of Sem Terra have been subject to increasingly violent attacks by mercenaries hired by landowners as well as federal and state forces who have also imprisoned high profile Sem Terra activists.

situationism Hybrid of autonomist Marxism, surrealism and existentialism associated with French radicals, Guy Debord and Raoul Vaneigem. Like autonomism, situationism rejects revolutionary parties and vanguards, holding that revolutionary moments are not manufactured, but distinct 'events' in which otherwise suppressed desires, frustrations and creativity can break loose, in turn creating the conditions in which 'self-organisation' can become a reality. Situationists stress the necessity for a popular counter-aesthetic to capitalism, ideas which can be found today in the outlook and activities of 'adbusting' and 'subvertising'.

social democracy Term initially associated with the German and Austrian socialists of the late nineteenth century who followed an electoral and parliamentary strategy – as opposed to the revolutionary strategy urged by figures such as Lenin. Social democracy is now associated with the idea of making market economies work to the benefit of the many rather than the few. This is achieved through state intervention to promote economic growth and redistribution to ensure social equality and welfare provision. Global social democrats such as David Held and George Monbiot envisage a similar model operating on a global basis through the extension of the political authority of existing and future institutions.

Subcomandante Insurgente Marcos Leading thinker, poet and philosopher of the Zapatistas which since 1994 has fought off the Mexican federal army in the Chiapas region. Marcos is associated with 'Zapatismo', which rejects conventional revolutionary doctrine, the idea of the vanguard party and the 'leading role' of intellectuals in anticapitalist struggles. Many of his speeches and writings are collected in *The Word is Our Weapon*.

via campesina A 'real' and virtual network of peasant and agriculturally based groups across the developing world in particular. Campaigns in favour of sustainable and equitable agriculture, against the patenting of crops and GM foods. Members also lobby against large scale agro-industrial developments generally, in favour of small scale, 'family' and community based farming.

WOMBLES White Overalls Movement Building Libertarian Effective Struggles – loosely constituted and autonomistically inclined grouping specialising in non-violent but confrontational direct action at major protests alongside Ya Basta! and Tuti Bianchi.

world bank Set up alongside the IMF as part of the Bretton Woods settlement at the end of the Second World War. Finances development and reconstruction projects. A focus for protests because of the harsh terms set for repayment of loans which often leave already impoverished nations even poorer.

world economic forum Normally meeting in Davos, Switzerland on an annual basis. The WEF is a private association paid for by the subscriptions of large corporations. It promotes 'dialogue', largely among the wealthy, though speakers from the developing world are usually invited as well. It acts as an informal lobbying group urging national governments and global institutions to promote the private sector and corporate interests generally.

world social forum (WSF) An initiative launched in 2000 (first meeting in January 2001) by members of ATTAC and the Brazilian Workers' Party to provide an alternative viewpoint on global affairs to the WEF. Has since mushroomed into a vast anti-capitalist carnival meeting every January. Has also spawned regional and national social forums around the world, which similarly meet on an annual basis. Some suggest that the WSF becomes the basis for a more formally organised movement thereby filling the vacuum that currently exists in many countries caused by the rightward drift of existing socialist and social democratic parties.

world trade organisation (WTO) Set up in 1995 to give an institutional focus for the *General Agreement on Tariffs and Trade* negotiations which have been on-going since the Second World War. The object of the negotiations is the development of a 'level playing field' for global trade, the idea being that increased trade will lead to increased wealth across the globe (otherwise known as 'trickle down theory'). In theory, each nation has an equal voice in negotiations. In practice, decisions are usually arrived at between the major industrial countries (G8 +) before the meetings take place or at meetings (in the 'green room'). A major focus for anti-capitalist demonstrations because of the manner in which the North has successively protected its own interests at the cost of the developing world through 'trickle-up' measures such as the dumping of subsidised goods, gene patenting and preferential trading arrangements between wealthy nations.

ya basta! Italian autonomist grouping formed in the wake of the Zapatista uprising to provide a focus for efforts at promoting solidarity with struggles in the developing world. They have taken the lead at many major protests to coordinate direct action and non-violent confrontations with the authorities.

zapatistas (EZLN) The army of national liberation that took over the Chiapas region in the wake of the 1994 signing of the North America Free Trade Area (NAFTA) agreement. Since 1994 the Zapatistas have established a zone of forty or so communities which run on a directly democratic basis. They have also sought to broaden their struggle and are frequent participants in pan-American and global 'convergences'.

contemporary anti-capitalism: a timeline

Please note that the following represents a highly selective list of recent events to give readers some idea of how major events and initiatives mentioned in the book relate to each other chronologically. A much more extensive listing with links to reports, photos and relevant websites is maintained by People's Global Action at: www.nadir.org/nadir/initiativ/agp/en/

1998

May   Meeting of WTO in Geneva and 'M16' (for May 16) Day of Action.

October   Paris Citizens Summit Against the Multilateral Agreement on Investment (MAI).

1999

June   'Cologne99' EU and G8 Summit J18 (June 18) Global Day of Action – extensive demonstrations and marches around the world.

December   WTO Ministerial meeting in **Seattle** – N30 Global Action Day – 'The Turtles and Teamsters' march – street battles – (media) birth of the anti-capitalist/ anti-globalisation movement.

2000

April   Meeting of the IMF and World Bank in **Washington, DC** to discuss structural adjustment policies and austerity measures for Mexico and Haiti – large demonstrations.

June   Meeting of the Organisation of American States in Windsor, Ontario – demonstrations and large numbers arrested. Demonstrations in Millau, France against the arrest of José Bové and others for wrecking a McDonald's restaurant – debates and workshops.

September   World Economic Forum meets in **Melbourne**, Australia – S11 Day of Action – massive demonstrations. Meeting of the IMF in **Prague** – S26 Global Day of Action – extensive street battles.

December   EU Summit in **Nice** – massive demonstrations.

2001

January   Meeting of the World Economic Forum in Davos, Switzerland shadowed by meeting of the first World Social Forum (WSF) in Porto Alegre, Brazil, hosted by Brazilian Workers' Party and French journal *Le Monde Diplomatique.*

March   Zapatistas march to Mexico City demanding rights for indigenous groups and resolution of the land question.

April   WTO Meeting in **Quebec City**, Canada – A20 Global Day of Action against 'Summit of the Americas' – extensive arrests and violence against protesters.

June   World Bank Meeting in **Barcelona** – cancelled due to threat of 'disorder'. Street parties and demonstrations take place anyway.

July   G8 Meeting in **Genoa** – One of the most violent protests since the new wave of activism – protester Carlo Guiliani shot dead and run over by police van.

September   '9/11': World Bank and IMF Meetings cancelled.

November   WTO Meeting in **Qatar** to discuss intellectual property rights (the 'Doha Round').

2002

January   Meeting of WEF in New York with extensive demonstrations and protests; Second WSF Meeting at Porto Alegre, Brazil.

April   Meeting of World Bank and IMF in **Washington, DC** – A20 Day of Action – extensive demonstrations.

June   G8 Summit in **Kananaskis, Canada** – despite extreme remoteness of location there are still demonstrations.

August   Foro Social Mundial, Argentina – anti-globalisation convergence to discuss strategies to confront austerity measures.

September	World Bank and IMF Meetings in **Washington, DC** – S26 Day of Action.
October	International Indigenous Day in Latin America – convergence to discuss shared problems of indigenous groups and strategies to confront elites. O20 Day of Action in Latin America – extensive demonstrations in **Quito** and elsewhere. Global Day of Action Against War – 'Not in Our Name' marches across the world. Encuentro Continental in Equador: 'Another America is Possible'.
November	First European Social Forum, Italy. WTO Meeting in Sydney, Australia – demonstrations 'Buy Nothing Day'.
December	Global Day of Action for Argentina – demonstrations and marches across the world.

2003

January	First Asian Social Forum, Hyderabad, India. Third WSF, Porto Alegre, Brazil.
April	Mobilisation against US Intervention in Latin America and the Caribbean, Washington, DC. Meetings of the World Bank and IMF, Washington, DC – demonstrations. First Oceania Social Forum, New Zealand.
June	G8 Summit **Evian**, France – Day of Action – extensive demonstrations. EU Summit, Greece – extensive demonstrations.
July	South Asian Peasants' Assembly – massive convergence to discuss regional strategy of resistance.
August	'Larzac 2003': Extensive anti-capitalist festival organised by *Confédération Paysanne* near Millau, France.
September	Global Week of Action against the WTO. Fifth WTO Ministerial, **Cancun**, Mexico. Major demonstrations across the world. Suicide of Korean farmer, Lee Kyung-hae.
October	Second Oceania Social Forum, Wellington, New Zealand.
November	Second European Social Forum, Paris, France.

2004

January	Fourth WSF, India.

index